Effective Writing

Writing skills for
intermediate students of
American English

Student's Book

Jean Withrow

CAMBRIDGE
UNIVERSITY PRESS

PUBLISHED BY THE PRESS SYNDICATE OF THE UNIVERSITY OF CAMBRIDGE
The Pitt Building, Trumpington Street, Cambridge, United Kingdom

CAMBRIDGE UNIVERSITY PRESS
The Edinburgh Building, Cambridge CB2 2RU, UK   http://www.cup.cam.ac.uk
40 West 20th Street, New York, NY 10011–4211, USA   http://www.cup.org
10 Stamford Road, Oakleigh, Melbourne 3166, Australia
Ruiz de Alarcón 13, 28014 Madrid, Spain

First published 1987
Tenth printing 1999

Printed in the United States of America

Typeset in Sabon

Library of Congress Cataloging-in-Publication Data

Withrow, Jean, 1937–
Effective writing.
Summary: A practice book for achieving writing skills
in American English in such areas as letters, stories,
reports, articles, instructions, business letters,
memos, and opinion essays.
1. English language – Rhetoric. 2. English language–
Text-books for foreign speakers. [1. English language–
Rhetoric. 2. English language – Textbooks for foreign
speakers] I. Title
PE1408.W6236 1987   808′.042   86–32659

ISBN 0-521-31608-1 (student's book)
ISBN 0-521-31609-X (teacher's manual)

Contents

Acknowledgments

The author and publisher are grateful to those who have given permission for the use of copyrighted material in the text:

UPI/Bettmann Newsphotos for the photographs on pp. 4, 34, 83; Peter Kneebone for the illustration on p. 11; Cinecom International Films and Island Alive for the still from *El Norte* (© Cinecom Pictures 1983) on p. 13; Marc P. Anderson for the first three photographs (from left to right) and Joseph Greene for the remainder of the photographs on p. 17; AP/Wide World Photos for the photographs on pp. 33, 72 *(right);* American Airlines for the advertisement on p. 37; Louis Inturrisi for the article on which Exercise 5.2 on p. 46 is based; Data General and Stoen Photos, Inc., for the photograph on p. 58; Casia Chalas for the essay on p. 67; Joseph Greene for the photograph on p. 70 *(left);* New York Convention and Visitors Bureau for the photograph on p. 70 *(right);* Pennsylvania Bureau of Travel Development for the photograph on p. 72 *(left);* Marc P. Anderson for the photograph on p. 74; Margaret Aristide for the essay "Poor People and Nutrition" on p. 76; Reuters/Bettmann Newsphotos for the photograph on p. 79; *The Observer* for the photograph on p. 84.

Illustrations by Bryan Hendrix: pp. 14, 46
Illustrations by Elivia Savadier-Sagov: pp. 18, 73
Illustration by Mary Jo Quay: p. 27

Book design by Peter Ducker
Cover design by Frederick Charles Ltd.

To the student

Effective Writing is a book that helps you gain some of the skills you need when you write in English. The aim of the book is to help you recognize what good writing is and to give you practice writing complete, cohesive paragraphs and compositions. The purpose, in short, is to help you make what you write more effective.

Here are some of the reasons that a piece of writing is ineffective, or difficult for a reader to understand:

1. The ideas are not in an **order** that makes sense; the piece is not **well-organized.**

2. The ideas are not grouped together into **paragraphs.**

3. The writer does not start the piece with a **beginning** that starts the reader in the right direction.

4. The writer does not finish the piece with an **ending** that leaves the reader with a sense of completion.

5. The **relation** between the ideas is not clear because the writer has not used words like *for example, on the other hand, because,* and so on.

6. The writer's **attitude** is not clear. Is the writer, for example, describing, suggesting, or criticizing something?

7. The piece contains ideas that are not **relevant** to what the writer wants to express.

8. The sentences do not have clear **punctuation;** there are commas (,) and periods (.) without any good reason.

The material in this book practices all these aspects of good writing. Obviously, different students vary in what they do well and what they need to work on, and they therefore need to concentrate on different things. This material allows you to do that; you can vary the order and type of exercises to suit your needs.

Many of the instructions given for the exercises suggest that you work with a group. You can learn a great deal by working with others to solve a problem or make a decision. Group work is a way of sharing knowledge, comparing opinions, and discussing ideas orally before doing individual or class work. However, this way of working is only a suggestion. Different teachers and classes should feel free to adjust any of the suggestions about ways of working with the material to suit their own needs and circumstances.

1 Formal and informal letters

ORGANIZING IDEAS

Read this help-wanted ad:

> ## TRAVEL AGENT
> Bright individual with good phone manner, varied duties, must type 60 wpm, bilingual a plus. Experience preferred.
> Send resume: F3140 Times.

The following sentences form a letter that answers this ad, but the sentences are in the wrong order. Working in groups, put them in logical order. Discuss how the underlined words help you.

Should the letter be divided into paragraphs? If so, where?

```
                                    4831 East 6th Street
                                    Los Angeles, California 90037
                                    June 3, 1988



Ms. Maria Cuellar
Travel Agents International
P.O. Box 3974
Los Angeles, California 90031


Dear Ms. Cuellar:
```

a) My primary responsibility <u>at Vacations Plus</u> was helping plan international trips for individuals and groups.

b) I <u>therefore</u> feel confident that I can make a contribution to your company.

c) I enclose a resume as requested, and I <u>look forward to hearing from you</u> at your earliest convenience.

1

d) In reference to your advertisement in the <u>Times</u> June 1, I would like to apply for the position of travel agent.

e) <u>Additional</u> <u>duties</u> included typing correspondence, doing ticketing, and telephoning airlines, bus companies, and clients.

f) In <u>dealing</u> <u>with</u> <u>clients</u>, I was often required to use Spanish and French, both of which I speak fluently.

g) I have an Associate of Arts degree in Travel and Tourism and have worked as an intern at Vacations Plus Travel Company.

Sincerely yours,

Gerard Gernand

Gerard Gernand

1.2   RELATING IDEAS: LINKING WORDS AND PHRASES

In groups, discuss the linking words and phrases underlined in paragraph 1 of the letter below. What do they mean? How do they link ideas? How are they punctuated?

Then, working individually or in groups, choose the best word or phrase for each blank in paragraphs 2 and 3 from the list below the letter.

Dear Reynaldo,

Do you remember I told you I was trying to get a part-time job as a waiter at a Japanese restaurant? (1) <u>Well</u>, I finally managed to get one! Of course, I haven't been working there long, (2) <u>but</u> I can already tell it's a wonderful place to work. All the staff, even the maître d', are very friendly. (3) <u>Besides</u>, the pay is pretty good, (4) <u>and</u> they let us eat whatever we want after work. (5) <u>For instance</u>, last night I had a big platter of sushi at 11:00!

I work only as a dinner waiter (6)........................ I go to classes during the day. My main job is to take orders from customers, give the orders to the cooks, (7)........................ take the food to the customers. I often have to describe the different Japanese dishes, (8)........................ sashimi, sukiyaki, or teriyaki. Sometimes Japanese customers speak to

*me in Japanese, expecting me to know the language.
(9).........................., I know only a few words of Japanese,
(10)......................... I get a little embarrassed. You know, my
grandparents immigrated from Japan, (11)........................... my
parents never taught me Japanese. I'm pretty well over
my embarrassment now, (12)........................, and am
taking advantage of learning more of the language on
the job. I find the job very interesting
(13)....................... I get to meet so many different
people.
(14)........................., that's my news. What about
you? Drop me a line when you have time. Regards to
your family.*

as always,

Ken

6. a) because   b) by the way   c) however
7. a) and   b) so   c) for instance
8. a) besides   b) however   c) such as
9. a) then   b) however   c) although
10. a) then   b) so   c) because
11. a) because   b) besides   c) but
12. a) well   b) though   c) and
13. a) why   b) because   c) then
14. a) well   b) for example   c) but

Put a linking word or phrase in each blank below so that the relationship between the statements is clear. Choose from these words:

such as   besides   however
but   because   and

15. There are a lot of advantages to this job. For one thing, the pay and working
    conditions are good. _____, it's only five minutes' walk from
    where I live.

16. I didn't apply for that other job _____ I didn't think I had
    much chance of getting it.

17. A lot of working groups, _____ plumbers, electricians, and
    teachers, have unions that protect their members' rights.
    _____ , waiters and waitresses do not.

18. At first I didn't feel happy about not having a union, _____
    now it doesn't bother me.

1.3   SHOWING ATTITUDE

Fill in the blanks below with words and phrases that show the writer's attitude toward what he is saying. Choose the best expression for each from those given below the letter.

Dear Editor:

    I am responding to last week's editorial, "Youth: Our Nation's Future," in which you praised the young people of today. (1) _____, there are just as many teenagers today who deserve praise, but there are just as many who, (2) _____, deserve no praise whatsoever.

    Take, for example, the gangs of kids that hang out on the streets of our town every night until the early hours of the morning. They not only dress strangely; they also behave irresponsibly. I have seen them write on store windows and walls. I have seen them push over parking meters and young trees. (3) _____, I have even seen them throwing stones and yelling at elderly people walking by! (4) _____, these kinds of youngsters deserve, not praise, but reprimand and punishment. (5) _____, that is not what they are getting. The police do their best to control these disrespectful young people, but, (6) _____, a handful of policemen cannot be everywhere at once.

    I can suggest one solution to this problem of misbehaving teenagers, and that is, (7) _____, why I am writing - to make my proposal known. I suggest a 9 p.m. curfew

for kids under 18, unless, (8) _____, they are
accompanied by an adult. (9) _____, this
nightly curfew will not solve all of the problems caused by
disrespectful youths, but it will, I believe, solve some of them.

James Pollack

Choose from these:

1. a) admittedly   b) personally   c) eventually
2. a) in theory   b) in my opinion   c) fortunately
3. a) obviously   b) in fact   c) naturally
4. a) officially   b) unofficially   c) clearly
5. a) unfortunately   b) decidedly   c) fortunately
6. a) obviously   b) to my surprise   c) seriously
7. a) frankly   b) by all means   c) personally
8. a) in fact   b) to be honest   c) of course
9. a) to my surprise   b) naturally   c) fortunately

1.4   USING REPORTING WORDS

Look at these ways of reporting what someone said.

a) "I'm going to the movies on Friday," said Jose.
   Jose said he was going to the movies on Friday.

b) "Will you go to the movies with me on Friday?" said Jose to Sara.
   Jose asked Sara if she would go to the movies with him on Friday.

c) "Sure, I'll go to the movies with you on Friday," said Sara.
   Sara said she would go to the movies with him on Friday.

d) "I'm not going to the movies on Friday," Ellen said to Jose.
   Ellen told Jose she wasn't going to the movies on Friday.

Notice how the underlined words change in the examples above when the sentences are rewritten using the reporting words ASK, SAY, and TELL.

The following sentences are given in the form of direct speech. Change each sentence into reported speech by using the word in parentheses at the end of the sentence. The first sentence is done for you as an example.

1. "I'm going to have a party next Saturday night," said Sam. (say)
   Sam said he was going to have a party next Saturday night.
2. "I'm going to be out of town that weekend," said Fran to Sam. (tell)
3. "I'll come!" said Henry. (say)
4. "Is there anything you want me to bring?" said Henry. (ask)
5. "Sure, would you like to bring a bottle of wine?" said Sam. (ask)
6. "Fran, I'm sorry you can't come," said Henry. (say)

5

1.5 WRITING FIRST AND LAST SENTENCES

A. *The first and last sentences of the following letter are missing. Work individually or in groups. Choose the best sentences from those given below the letter. Decide what makes a good first sentence and a good last sentence.*

P.O. Box 160
Harvard, Massachusetts 01451
June 24, 1988

Lost and Found
TWA
Logan International Airport
Boston, Massachusetts 02128

Dear Lost and Found Department,

. . . .

. . . .

I had the wallet when I boarded flight #753 in London at 10:45 a.m. on June 23. When I tried to pay for a taxi in Boston, however, I discovered it was missing. Therefore, I conclude that I must have dropped it on the plane somewhere during the trip. The wallet is beige leather, and it contained several credit cards in my name, as well as about US $140 in cash. I traveled in the nonsmoking section, in the second row from the front.

. . . .

. . . .

Sincerely yours,
Lucia de la Cruz
Lucia de la Cruz

Choices for first sentence:

a. My wallet, which I seem to have lost, was a present from my husband.
b. Some people keep money in a pocket, but I prefer to keep it in my good-quality wallet.
c. Do you have my wallet by any chance?
d. I am writing to you to ask about my wallet, which I lost yesterday.

Choices for last sentence:

a. Some time ago I lost a chain on one of your planes, and on that occasion you were kind enough to return it to me.
b. I would be very grateful if you could let me know if it has been turned in to you.
c. If I found somebody else's wallet, I would most definitely turn it in to the Lost and Found Department.
d. I am sure you find hundreds of wallets every day, but if you look carefully, you might find mine.

B. *Now decide what the main purpose of the following letter is, and write a suitable first sentence and last sentence for it.*

10 Washington Street
Marblehead, Massachusetts 01945
June 25, 1988

Dear Ms. de la Cruz,

....
....

I found it on the TWA plane that flew from London to Boston on June 23 (flight #753). It was on the floor in front of seat 2C.

Because the wallet contains credit cards and cash, I hesitate to mail it to you...
....
....

Sincerely yours,

John Tavera

1.6   **COMPARING TEXTS: ORGANIZING**

A. Below are two applications for a scholarship to study at a university in the United States. Either individually or in a group, decide which is better organized and more appropriately written. Discuss your decision and reasons with others.

Letter 1:

Dear Financial Aid Office,

    I would like to apply for a university scholarship to study civil engineering at your university, starting next September. I am in my final year of a 5-year degree course in engineering at Munich University. In our last two years we have to choose an optional subject, and I have opted for civil engineering with a specialization in city planning. I worked from July to September of last year and the year before as a volunteer in the office of the Munich City Council.

    My reading has included many articles and reports, several of which were from the United States and Great Britain, on traffic-free shopping centers. This particular aspect of city planning interests me because the centers of many German towns suffer from the dense traffic. Because your university is in the forefront of work in this area, I would like very much to do my postgraduate work there.

    I look forward to hearing from you.

Sincerely yours,

Hans Namberger

Letter 2:

Dear Financial Aid Office,

The U.S.A. is where things are happening in my
particular field. I have very little experience, but my
degree allows for the specialization in the planning of city
centers. As far as I can see, your university would be a
good place to study. At the end of this year my course will
end, and I would like to go on studying traffic-free city
centers. I have worked in the office of the Munich City
Council, but only part-time. I should say that my degree is
in civil engineering.

Several of the reports which I have read were produced
in the United States and Great Britain, and traffic is a big
problem in the center of many German towns, too. If I could
study, say for one year, then that would continue my
optional subject. The period of study I'm interested in
could be any time starting next September, because my 5-year
degree course in civil engineering ends at Munich University
this summer.

I was not paid while I was working (from July to
September) in the planning office, but I would like to do
postgraduate work in the same field. I understand that your
university has experts in the field of traffic-free shopping
centers, and I would like to apply for a scholarship to
study there.

That's all for now.

Rupert Bormann

Rupert Bormann

B. *Now write a letter of application for a scholarship based on the information below.*
   You do not need to use all of the information. You may add more details if you
   wish.

Name	Anna Peterson
Address	15 Washington Street
	Hoboken, New Jersey 07030
Date of birth	31 March 1963; Walton, New York
Degree	B.A. June 1985, State University of New York,
	Binghamton, N.Y.
Major	Business
Present position	Since June 1985, Legal Services, Newark, New Jersey
Current work	Paralegal work with emphasis on tenants' rights and
	immigration law
Other experience	Volunteer at St. John's Church, Hoboken, in community legal
	assistance program (2 years)
Goal	To attend Brooklyn Law School as a part-time student and
	study for a degree in law

1.7   PUNCTUATING: APOSTROPHES AND CAPITAL LETTERS

A. *In groups, discuss the use of the apostrophe (') in the following:*

It's mine.   You're wrong.   He can't come.   We'd better go.
Maria's sister has come.   The children's toys are gone.
All the students' names were read.

There are apostrophes in the sentences below. Some are used correctly, and some are not. Correct the incorrectly used apostrophes.

1. You'll never believe whose car I rode in last week – Margarets!
2. Ill be honest; it's not really her's.
3. It's her parent's.
4. But Margarets learning to drive, and I'am always willing to go for a ride in a new car.
5. Were still laughing about Margarets' attempts to parallel park!

B. *Discuss why capital letters are used in these expressions:*

1. Ms. Moreno, Carol Morley, Dr. Orange, the Prime Minister, the Bishop of Calcutta
2. Sixth Avenue, Bouchart Gardens, Lake Constance, the Delaware River, the Museum of Modern Art, the Hilton Hotel
3. Monday, Tuesday, January, March, Christmas, New Year's Day
4. English, Hindi, Spanish, Indian, Spaniard, Colombian

C. *Now put apostrophes and capital letters where necessary in the following letter:*

dear miriam and paul,
    thank you for having tony and me for the weekend.
we had a great time, especially at the dinner party
saturday night. wed never had a real thai dinner
before, and now we cant wait for our next one! tony
especially liked the frogs legs with peanut sauce. in
fact, when we got home, he went out into the yard to
try to catch some frogs. hes out there every night
after work. i dont know what he thinks were going to
do with them once theyre caught because im sure not
going to cook them!
    we also enjoyed the tour around town on sunday and
our visit to the museum of modern art. our walk along
the river at sundown was the perfect end to a great day.
    we hope youll come to visit us soon. theres a lot

to do here, too, and well plan a big weekend. theres a wonderful museum with a large collection of indian art that im sure youll find interesting. didnt you say you were free in november? why dont you come then?

thanks again

Maria

1.8   PRACTICING WRITING LETTERS

Choose one of the following topics. Write:

a) A letter of application for a job of your choice. (Compare 1.1)
b) A letter about a new job or a new course of studies. (Compare 1.2)
c) A letter responding to Mr. Pollack's letter in 1.3 objecting to his suggestion or disagreeing with his viewpoint about teenagers.
d) A letter to the editor of a local newspaper giving your opinion about an article or editorial you recently read or about an issue, such as whether service in the military should be required or on a volunteer basis. Give as many reasons for your viewpoint as possible. (Compare 1.3)
e) A letter to a place inquiring about something you lost or reporting something you found. (Compare 1.5)
f) A letter of application to a specific school for a scholarship to do further studies in your field or to a specific business or company for an internship in your field of work. (Compare 1.6)
g) A letter to friends thanking them for a recent visit. (Compare 1.7)
h) A letter reporting on the experiences of a person you know who has recently done something difficult or interesting.
i) A letter to an appropriate official protesting something that is planned for your neighborhood or community.

2 Writing a story

2.1   ORGANIZING IDEAS

The following sentences form the opening paragraph of a story, but they are in the wrong order. Working with a group, put them in logical order. Discuss how the underlined words and phrases help you.

a) <u>Finally</u> she reached bottom. 9
b) Burning with curiosity, she jumped up to follow <u>it</u>. 3
c) So she <u>did</u>, and found that <u>the liquid</u> had a very pleasant flavor. 7
d) Suddenly a white rabbit ran by <u>her</u>, saying to itself, "Oh dear! I shall be too late!" 2
e) <u>But</u> as she <u>drank</u>, something curious happened – she began to shrink! 8
f) <u>It</u> was a long <u>hole</u>, and she <u>fell</u> for such a long time that she thought she might fall through to the other side of the earth. 5
g) The <u>rabbit</u> went down a hole, and she jumped in after it. 4
h) <u>There</u> she saw a bottle with a label that said, "DRINK ME." 6
i) Alice was beginning to get very tired of sitting in the field having nothing to do. 1

2.2   RELATING IDEAS: LINKING WORDS AND PHRASES

A. *In groups, discuss the linking words and phrases underlined in the story below. What do they mean? How do they link ideas? How are they punctuated?*

> nting. Did I tell you about the rock band I'm in? We've only been together about three months. Well, the other band members wanted us to enter this music contest. (1) <u>At first</u>, I didn't think we were good enough. Then we played at a couple of parties, and people seemed to like

us, so (2) <u>finally</u> I said OK. The judges took ages to make up their minds, and we were so nervous we could hardly wait. But then the head judge came onto the stage. (3) "<u>At last!</u>" I whispered to my neighbor. We were pretty amazed — we didn't win first place, but we came in second!

B. *In the movie review below, the linking words and phrases are missing. Working in groups, choose the most appropriate word or phrase from those given below the review.*

MOVIE REVIEW

El Norte

"El Norte" is an excellent and disturbing film about two immigrants to the United States. (4) _____ _____ of the film we meet a family in Guatemala – mother, father, son, and daughter. When the father is killed and the mother is taken to prison, the son and daughter decide to go to "El Norte" – the United States – by way of Mexico. (5) _____, they have trouble finding someone to take them across the Mexican border, but (6) _____ they find a way across and end up in Los Angeles. (7) _____, life in the U.S. is not as easy as they thought it would be. (8) _____, they have to find housing. (9) _____ they need to learn English and get jobs. (10) _____ they succeed in accomplishing these three goals, and life looks pretty good for them. Unfortunately, (11) _____ of the film, tragedy strikes, and we are left wondering if "El Norte" really is the land of opportunity after all.

4. a) first   b) at the beginning   c) at first
5. a) at first   b) however   c) finally
6. a) on the other hand   b) finally   c) second
7. a) for example   b) besides   c) however
8. a) at the end   b) such as   c) first
9. a) third   b) then   c) but
10. a) unfortunately   b) eventually   c) for instance
11. a) finally   b) at the end   c) last

2.3   USING REPORTING WORDS

Notice these different ways to report what someone said:

"Oh, dear, I'm afraid I've made a big mistake," said Eva.
a) Eva <u>said</u> she had made a big mistake.
b) Eva <u>admitted</u> (that) she had made a big mistake.
c) Eva <u>thought</u> (that) she had made a big mistake.
d) Eva <u>announced</u> (that) she had made a big mistake.

How do the underlined words change the meaning of what is reported?

Notice that the reporting words ADMITTED, THOUGHT, and ANNOUNCED give an idea of what Eva said and HOW she said it without using all of her words. SAID tells what she said, but not how she said it. Notice also the change in verb tense.

The following sentences are given in the form of direct speech. Change each sentence into reported speech by using the word in parentheses at the end of the sentence.

1. "Oh dear, I'm afraid I've made a big mistake," said Eva. (think)
2. "You see, I've just typed eleven pages of my story on the computer – and now it's disappeared!" said Eva. (explain)
3. "It's true, I forgot to press the save key, and all because I was so involved in my story," said Eva. (admit)
4. "Unfortunately, I don't think there's any way to get it back again," said Eva. (doubt)
5. "I tell you, no matter what people say, computers are *not* more efficient than typewriters!" said Eva. (insist)
6. "I have some advice for people writing on a computer: They should press the save key, and press it *often*," said Eva. (suggest)

2.4   WRITING FIRST AND LAST SENTENCES

A. The first and last sentences of the following story are missing. Working individually or in groups, choose the best first and last sentence from those below the story. Decide what makes a good first sentence and a good last sentence.

. . . .

. . . .

A few years ago I spent a week in the Dominican Republic. The week was over, and I was at the airport ready to leave when I discovered, to my dismay, that I had forgotten one of my suitcases at my hotel. Quickly, I jumped into a taxi and explained my situation to the taxi driver. We sped off in the direction of my hotel. Suddenly, the taxi driver slowed down so he could talk with the driver of a truck moving along the road next to us. The truck contained live chickens. Without stopping the taxi, the taxi driver stuck his hand out the window and took a live chicken, which he neatly stuck under the seat next to him. Meanwhile, I was getting more and more anxious about my suitcase and making my plane on time. Time wasn't bothering the taxi driver, though. Instead of heading straight for the hotel, he made a detour to drop the chicken off at his home! In the end, however, we managed to get the suitcase and then raced back to the airport. Fortunately, I made it to my plane on time.

. . . .

. . . .

Choices for first sentence:

a) There are lots of things to do in the Dominican Republic if you have enough time.
b) Traveling can have its exciting, though frustrating, moments.
c) I've always enjoyed traveling.
d) I often go to the Dominican Republic, and I always take a taxi from the airport to my hotel.

Choices for last sentence:

a) That was the second time I'd been to the Dominican Republic; the first time was eight years ago.
b) Airline connections to the Dominican Republic are fairly good.
c) Travel is a difficult thing.
d) What started out as a frustrating moment ended up being a hilarious memory and a great story.

⟫→

15

B. Now, working individually or in groups, complete the following paragraph. The first and last sentences are given.

```
But the best thing about the vacation was the people we met

by accident on the beach ....................................

.............................................................

.............................................................

.............................................................

.............................................................

................... That should give you some idea why we

had such a good time together.
```

2.5   COMPARING TEXTS: SENTENCE CONNECTIONS

Below are two versions of a story. Decide which story uses better sentence connections (linking words and phrases) and more variety in sentence types. Discuss your answer and reasons with others.

A. He immigrated to the United States in the late 1800s. He and his wife settled in the Pacific Northwest. They had three children. His wife died. He went back to Italy, he went to look for another wife, and he took the children with him. He got to Italy. The woman he wanted to marry had left for this country. He and the children returned to the United States. He followed the woman to a small town in New York state. Finally he convinced her to marry him, they settled in New York and had five children, and my mother was one of them. The woman my grandfather crossed the Atlantic Ocean twice for was my grandmother.

B. In the late 1800s, a man immigrated to the United States. He and his wife settled in the Pacific Northwest and soon had three children. Unfortunately, his wife died. After her death, the man, with the children, went back to Italy to look for another wife. When he got there, he discovered that the woman he wanted to marry had recently left for the United States, so he and the children returned to this country, following the woman to a small town in New York state. After finally convincing the woman to marry him, they settled on a farm there and eventually had five children. My mother was one of them. The woman my grandfather crossed the Atlantic Ocean twice for was my grandmother.

Now write a story about someone in your family. Try to vary linking words and sentence types.

2.6   *WRITING TEXT BASED ON A VISUAL*

Working in groups of two or three, look at the following eight photographs, and choose at least six of them. Arrange them in an order that makes a good story. Discuss the development of the story in the group and invent any details that you need. Then, working individually, write the story.

2.7   PUNCTUATING: QUOTATION MARKS

A. Notice the punctuation in the following sentences:

1a. "Why do you walk so crookedly?" shouted an old crab to a young one.
 b. An old crab shouted to a young one, "Why do you walk so crookedly?"

2a. "Walk straight!" the old crab yelled.
 b. The old crab yelled, "Walk straight!"

3a. "Why don't you show me how?" replied the young crab sweetly.
 b. The young crab replied sweetly, "Why don't you show me how?"

4a. "When I see *you* walk straight, so will I," continued the young crab.
 b. The young crab continued, "When I see *you* walk straight, so will I."
 c. "When I see *you* walk straight," the young crab continued, "so will I."

 MORAL: Practice what you preach.

B. Now, working in groups, put punctuation marks and capital letters in these sentences:

5. Where are you going asked the rabbit
6. I announced the dog loudly am going to hunt rabbits
7. That's very nice the rabbit said quietly where will you find them
8. The dog replied knowingly there are dozens of them near the brook
9. Well the rabbit mumbled good luck in your hunting
10. Just a minute shouted the dog you look like you know something about rabbits
11. Yes I do the rabbit said in a soft voice
12. Tell me what you know the dog roared
13. I know enough whispered the rabbit as she hopped off into the bushes to recognize a good escape when I see one

 MORAL: Know what you're looking for.

2.8   PRACTICING WRITING STORIES

Choose one of the following topics. Write:

a) A summary of the plot (story) of a book (or part of a book) you have read or a movie you have seen. (Compare 2.1 and 2.2B)

b) The story of a competition or contest in which you or someone you know took part. (Compare 2.2A)

c) The story of a big mistake you made. (Compare 2.3)

d) The story of an incident that happened to you or someone you know during a trip or a vacation, or the story of a special day: a visit, a birthday, a wedding, an outing. (Compare 2.4)

e) A story about your family, or about a family ceremony or religious tradition. (Compare 2.5)

f) The story of something that happened to an older member of your family or to an older person you know. You may wish to interview the person first to get information and details to make an interesting story. (Compare 2.5)

g) A story (real or imaginary) based on a photograph or a series of photographs. (Compare 2.6) You may wish to use your own photos or those you find in newspapers or magazines.

h) A fable (compare 2.7), a folk tale, or an amusing story or joke.

3 Reports

3.1 **ORGANIZING IDEAS**

*The following sentences form a newspaper report, but they are in the wrong order.
Working in a group, put them in logical order. Discuss how the underlined words
help you. When you have finished, write the report out, dividing it into three or four
paragraphs. Discuss how you decided where to divide the story into paragraphs.*

Ship accident off West Coast of Canada

No Casualties

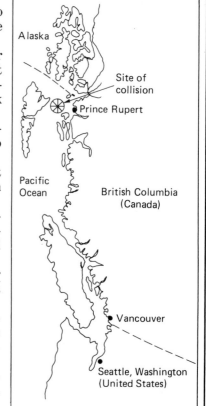

a) In spite of this damage, the two ships managed to reach Prince Rupert under their own steam.

b) However, because of the weather conditions, the captains did not realize the danger until a few seconds before the collision took place.

c) One was a cargo ship carrying lumber, apparently on its way to Prince Rupert.

d) The official added that government experts would be invited to join the committee.

e) Fortunately, there were no casualties among the crews or passengers, but both ships suffered damage close to the water line.

f) According to eyewitnesses, neither of the vessels was going very fast at the time of the accident.

g) Yesterday evening two boats collided in thick fog in the Pacific Ocean not far from Prince Rupert, British Columbia.

h) Consequently, there was insufficient time for them to prevent the accident.

i) | ³The other was a Canadian National ferry on its regular run from Vancouver to Prince Rupert.

j) | A spokesman for the port authorities said that a committee would be set up to determine the cause of the collision.

3.2   *RELATING IDEAS: LINKING WORDS AND PHRASES*

Below is a report written by a hotel inspector. Notice the linking words and phrases in paragraph 1. Discuss them with your group. What do they mean? How do they link ideas? How are they punctuated?

Then choose the best word or phrase for each blank from the list given below the report.

REPORT ON MY VISIT TO HOTEL DU LAC, JULY 3

(1) For the most part, I found things to be operating smoothly and efficiently. The staff seemed hard working and courteous. (2) For example, as soon as I checked in, (3) even though I was not identified as an inspector, a very polite porter was right there to take my luggage and escort me to my room. (4) In addition, the facilities and service were generally good, especially those connected with the front desk, the lobby, and the dining room.

(5) _____, I must report a few concerns. (6) _____, the elevator service was slow. This is not surprising, (7) _____, when you consider that there are only two elevators serving a hotel of sixteen floors.

(8) _____, the air conditioning in my room was difficult to adjust to a comfortable level. (9) _____ I asked for help, an engineer adjusted it for me. (10) _____, tools were needed to make the adjustment, (11) _____ I was unable to change the air temperature after that. I found similar problems in some of the other rooms, though not in all.

(12) _____, the carpeting on the main staircase was faded and worn. For aesthetic reasons (13) _____ for reasons of safety, it should be replaced.

I do not wish to give the impression that the hotel is operating

⟫→

improperly (14) _____ that it is in very poor condition. (15) _____, the service, staff, and facilities are, (16) _____, very good. If the problems mentioned in this report are corrected, the hotel will merit an excellent quality rating.

Choices:

5. a) however   b) for example   c) well   d) besides
6. a) first   b) at the beginning   c) in addition   d) well
7. a) even though   b) in fact   c) but   d) because
8. a) first   b) second   c) at last   d) and
9. a) even though   b) so   c) when   d) for instance
10. a) so   b) however   c) at first   d) because
11. a) because   b) so   c) finally   d) however
12. a) finally   b) second   c) for example   d) for the most part
13. a) even though   b) but   c) besides   d) as well as
14. a) or   b) because   c) so   d) even though
15. a) at last   b) on the contrary   c) well   d) when
16. a) finally   b) however   c) on the whole   d) for instance

---

3.3   *WRITING FIRST PARAGRAPHS*

A. *Below is a report to a company president from a committee of company workers about the feasibility of changing company work hours to flex-time. The report needs a first paragraph. Read the report and decide, either alone or in groups, which paragraph of those given below is best as a first paragraph and why. Look at both style and content.*

BC   BAYSIDE CORPORATION   **MEMO**

Subject: FEASIBILITY OF FLEXIBLE WORKING HOURS

(First paragraph missing) ....

The Personnel Manager was asked to look into the question, and his study had two aspects. First, he looked at the experience of other companies, and second, he looked carefully at our own working arrangements.

After studying flex-time arrangements at four similar companies, the Personnel Manager reported several advantages: Parents of school-age children were able to fit their work hours to those of their children, workers could choose to work during hours they could be most productive, and worker attitude improved because of more choice in work time. There were, however, some disadvantages as well: Sometimes there were not enough workers in some departments at crucial hours of the day, and it took a while to iron out confusion about schedules.

Next, we asked all employees of our company to predict the hours they would probably choose to work. This information was then circulated to all heads of department for comment. The department heads were asked to look in particular at possible problems and their solution.

After studying all this information, a committee that included a representative from every department decided to try flex-time for a period of 3 months, starting April 1. At the end of that period, the committee will make a final decision.

Choices for first paragraph:

a) We committee members have spent a lot of time investigating the question of hours. As you know, different people have different opinions about the idea. Because you get so many different opinions, it's not easy to make a final decision. But we have done what we think is right, and if people aren't completely happy, we hope they won't take our ideas personally.

b) Since 1984 everybody in this company has worked 40 hours per week. Before 1984, the total was 44 hours for some people and 42 for others. We have no intention of changing the 40-hour work week. Anyway, if the total number of work hours were to change, it would be possible only after negotiations between management and union representatives.

c) This report concerns the feasibility of allowing workers to start and stop work at the times that suit them best, a practice known as flex-time. Of course, we all understand that everyone would still work a total of 40 hours per week, as we do now. This idea of flexible working hours was first presented to the directors by some of our workers, many of whom have young children in school.

⫸→

B. Now read the report below, and then write an appropriate first paragraph.

Subject	FEASIBILITY OF SHORTENING SCHOOL TERM FROM 12 WEEKS TO 10 WEEKS

....

....

....

....

....

First, the director was asked to investigate the situation. The first thing she did was contact affiliated language schools in other cities that have tried a 10-week term instead of the usual 12-week term. Personnel at all of these schools had good things to say about the shorter semester: Student interest level remained high for the full 10-week period, students claimed they learned as much in 10 weeks as they did in 12 weeks, and teachers reported better than usual attendance. The shortened semester presented certain problems, however: Teachers said they had a hard time covering the same amount of material they had covered in a 12-week term, and students complained about having less time for extra activities, such as field trips and movies.

The second thing the director did, with the committee's help, was to ask both students and faculty here what they think of the plan, and especially what problems they foresee. The results of this inquiry were made known to faculty and students, as you know, and people were asked to suggest possible solutions to the problems posed.

Finally, the committee of faculty and student representatives examined this proposal. The committee decided that the advantages of a shorter semester outweigh the disadvantages. We have therefore decided to recommend trying out the plan for one term, the fall term of next year. Then the committee will make a final decision.

3.4   **USING REPORTING WORDS**

Compare these ways of reporting what someone said:

"I'll paint the window frames both outside and inside if you wish," said the contractor.

a) The contractor *said* he would paint the window frames both outside and inside if I wished.

b) The contractor *offered* to paint the window frames both outside and inside.

Notice that in (b) the word OFFERED tells what the contractor said and how he said it without using all of his exact words.

The following sentences are given in the form of direct speech. Change each sentence into reported speech by using the word in parentheses at the end of the sentence. The first sentence is done as an example.

1. "I'll do the best possible work on this job at the lowest price I can," said the contractor. (promise)
   The contractor promised to do the best possible work at the lowest price he could.
2. "I'll even throw in the paint at wholesale prices," said the contractor. (offer)
3. "I plan to finish the job by Friday if nothing goes wrong," he said. (intend)
4. "But if I can't, would it be OK to finish it up on Saturday?" said the contractor. (ask)
5. "I've never had a dissatisfied customer yet," he said. (boast)

3.5   *SELECTING AND ORDERING INFORMATION*

You have been asked to write a report on what is being done about overpopulation. The beginning of the report is written. Working in groups, decide which other points to include and why. Then group the points into paragraphs, adding linking words, phrases, and/or sentences where necessary. Finally, add a conclusion if needed.

A Report on Efforts to Control World Population: China, India, and Kenya

Many government leaders are coming to realize that population growth is reaching a crisis point; they feel that the world's land, water, and energy supplies will not be able to support many more people. This view, however, is often in opposition to the traditions and beliefs of many people. Consequently, conflicts often exist between government policies regarding birth control and people's practices. Looking at three specific countries, India, China, and Kenya, gives some insight into how effectively the world population crisis is being dealt with.

Other points to consider:

India's principal form of birth control today is sterilization.

In Africa, having many children is traditionally considered a gift, and having none, a great curse.

India's population will be near one billion by the year 2001; population growth is high, at 2.3 percent.

The Chinese government has imposed a policy of one child per family.

China tries to enforce its one-child policy with strong peer pressure, financial rewards for having only one child, and financial penalties for having more than one child.

Indian parents think that two sons and one daughter is the ideal small family, though the average family today has 4.3 children.

For religious reasons and because of custom, many Kenyans oppose birth control.

Kenya is one of seven African countries that have the world's highest population growth rate, at 4.1 percent.

The Indian government encourages families to have only two children.

The rate of infant deaths is high in India, so parents say, "One eye is no eyes, and one son is no sons."

Many Kenyans favor large families because they want to be supported in their old age.

Sons represent security in old age to Chinese parents.

For many people in Kenya, family planning clinics are far from their homes.

Family planning in India at present is voluntary.

Kenyan government officials encourage people to have fewer children and to use family planning.

Indian parents want sons so they will be cared for in old age.

It is not easy for China to administer a program of one child per family.

3.6   WRITING TEXT BASED ON A CONVERSATION

You have been staying at the apartment of friends while they are away. You arrived home last night to find the apartment burgled, and you had the following conversation with the police officer who came to investigate. Read the conversation, then write a letter to your friends telling them what happened. Before you start, list the points you will include. Remember to divide your letter into paragraphs.

P: Police officer. You reported a burglary?

A: Well, for a start, this isn't my place. I'm just staying here for two months while my friends are out of the city. So, besides the obvious things like radio, stereo, television set, and some paintings, I don't really know what else is missing. All the drawers have been emptied out and I suppose some things were taken, but I have no idea what. My friends will be furious!

P: I see. Now...

A: It wasn't my fault, of course. All the windows and doors were locked. I even left the hall light on to give the impression that someone was here. I just hope my friends won't hold me responsible.

P: Now, how exactly did you discover the burglary?

A: I went out at seven as I do every Thursday, to attend my computer class. Afterwards I stopped at the International Cafe for a drink, and I got back here just after eleven o'clock.

P: How can you be so sure of the time?

A: Because I was at the cafe till the ten o'clock news was over, and it's only a two-minute walk from here.

P: I see. And what did you find when you got back here?

A: This mess that you see here. And it's the same in the bedrooms – everything turned upside down, drawers emptied and things thrown around.

P: Do you know how the burglars got in?

A: Yes, the lock on the door has been forced.   ⫸→

P: Have you spoken to the neighbors? Maybe they saw or heard something.

A: No, I haven't. But the old man next door is almost deaf and sits in front of the TV all night, and the Lees, across the hall, are away.

P: How soon can you let us know exactly what's been taken?

A: I guess I'll have to write to my friends right away.

P: Yes, you should contact them immediately. We can't begin a full investigation until we know exactly what's missing.

A: Is there any chance of anything being recovered? I know my friends will be especially upset about the paintings.

P: We'll check for fingerprints and clues and then let you know. And if I were you, I'd write that letter right away.

3.7   *COMPARING TEXTS*

A. Below are two versions of a letter of recommendation for a person applying for a job. Working with a group, decide which version is more appropriate and why. Pay attention to relevance of information and sentence variety.

Version 1:

> I have been asked to write a letter of recommendation for Ms. Mariam Melaku. I am very pleased to do so. I have known Ms. Melaku since 1984; I was her faculty adviser and had her in several of my classes.
>
> Ms. Melaku is a very capable, creative person, one with integrity and a high sense of responsibility. She approaches a job with a great deal of enthusiasm, energy, and organizational ability. She has worked and lived in several countries and has always adapted readily to new cultures and environments. In addition, she speaks English and French fluently, along with her native language, Amharic. Ms. Melaku is a person who is knowledgeable about other cultures and is open to learning more. She relates extremely well to people of all ages and is sensitive and tactful in dealing with them.
>
> I recommend Ms. Melaku highly for a job requiring these skills.

Version 2:

I have been asked to write a letter of recommendation for Ms. Mariam Melaku. I'm glad to do it - she's a former student of mine. I have known her since 1984. We hit it off immediately, as soon as we met.

In my estimation, Ms. Melaku is one of the most capable, creative people I know. She has lots of integrity and a big sense of responsibility. She has a lot of enthusiasm, energy, and organizational ability. She's a lot of fun to be with. She speaks three languages like a native. The languages are French, Amharic, and English. Most important, Ms. Melaku is an expert on other cultures. She has lived in several countries. She adapts well to new cultures and environments. She relates well to people of all ages. She is sensitive and tactful in dealing with them. She has always treated me fairly.

I recommend her without hesitation to do any job for which she applies. I like her very much and wish her lots of luck in getting a job.

B. *Now write a letter of recommendation based on the information given below. You will need to explain and support each point in more detail. However, you do not need to include in your letter all of the information given.*

Name	George Isher
When and where you met	1981; worked as an intern with our company
Strengths	Pleasant person, easy-going
	Honest, responsible
	Works carefully and well, does jobs thoroughly
	Likes people, people like him
	Lots of fun to be with
	A good organizer, likes to set up systems
	Friendly
Skills	Knows computer programming, has taught use of computers
	Speaks Russian and English fluently, reads Spanish
	Types 80 words per minute accurately
	Pleasant telephone manner

3.8   WRITING TEXT BASED ON VISUAL INFORMATION

A. *The report below was written for a job supervisor. Read the report, relating it to the diagram on the right.*

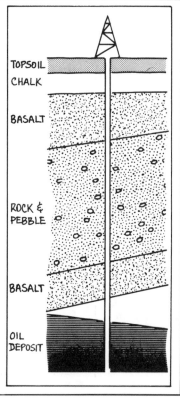

DRILLING CONDITIONS IN UJIKSHTAN

The first two or three feet were fairly easy to drill through, but after passing through a layer of chalk, we ran into our first layer of hard basalt. At this stage we had to change the drilling bit,* and as a result, the drilling became slower. As we went through this hard layer, we had to stop often to make sure that the bit was not getting too hot.

The third stage of the drilling was varied. Sometimes there were hard rocks or pebbles, and sometimes soft chalk. Although the ground was generally softer than the second layer, we could not go much faster because it was never soft for long, and changing the bits took a lot of time.

During the last stage we had to pass through even harder rock, and many times the drilling bit did overheat. However, through patience and some skillful work by the mechanics, we finally reached the oil deposits after we started drilling.

*drilling bit: the cutting part of a tool; the point of a drill

B. *Now, working alone or in groups, write a report that informs other drivers of the road conditions you experienced on a car trip from Bellevue to Ellensburg last week. Base your report on the diagram below.*

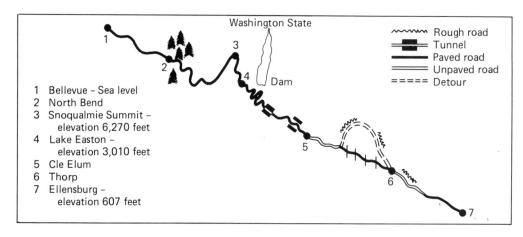

1 Bellevue – Sea level
2 North Bend
3 Snoqualmie Summit –
      elevation 6,270 feet
4 Lake Easton –
      elevation 3,010 feet
5 Cle Elum
6 Thorp
7 Ellensburg –
      elevation 607 feet

Washington State

Dam

Rough road
Tunnel
Paved road
Unpaved road
Detour

3.9   *PUNCTUATING: COMMAS*

A. *With your group, discuss the reasons for using commas in sentences 1–6 below:*

1. *Foreigner*, by Nahid Rachlin, is a novel about an Iranian woman caught between two cultures, those of her homeland, Iran, and her new country, the United States.
2. The setting of the story is modern-day Iran, and the heroine is a young Iranian woman named Feri.
3. In brief, the plot is as follows.
4. Feri, who has lived in the United States for 14 years and has married an American, returns to her homeland and finds herself in conflict with many things, including her family, memories of her childhood, Iranian customs and traditions, and Iranian beliefs about women and marriage.
5. While visiting her mother in a remote area of Iran, Feri becomes ill and meets a young Iranian doctor.
6. This experience causes her to ask herself such questions as, "Where do I belong?" and "Can my marriage last?"

B. *Now put commas in the appropriate places in the rest of the book report. You should have a good reason for every comma you use. Then compare your answers and discuss your reasons with others in your group.*

7. Although Feri never completely and finally answers these questions for herself or the reader, the novel ends with a resolution that at least for the moment satisfies the reader.
8. I recommend this novel highly not just because it deals with an experience common to many people, who have adopted a new country, but also because Ms. Rachlin has succeeded so well in making Feri's experiences and feelings real to us.
9. In fact, once I started reading the book, I couldn't put it down.
10. For one thing, Ms. Rachlin's ability to make every incident even the smallest contribute to the feeling of tension and conflict compelled me to read on to the end.
11. In addition, her expertise in describing the sights, smells, sounds, and tastes of Iran helped make me feel exactly what Feri felt.
12. Because I was very involved in her story, I wanted to know how it came out.
13. The fact that there were questions unanswered at the end of the novel may make some readers uncomfortable, but I didn't feel that way.
14. I liked making my own guesses and creating my own fantasies about Feri's future.
15. In short, I loved *Foreigner*.

3.10   **PRACTICING WRITING REPORTS**

Choose one of the following topics. Write:

a) A report on an accident you heard about or witnessed. (Compare 3.1)

b) A report recommending a new policy for your school or place of work. (Compare 3.3)

c) A report on a lecture, TV documentary, or radio talk you heard. (Compare 3.5)

d) A report, written either for the police or an insurance company, on a burglary, mugging, or accident that you saw or were a victim of. (Compare 3.6)

e) A letter recommending someone you know for a job or a school. (Compare 3.7)

f) A report to a job supervisor about a job you completed. If helpful, include a drawing to illustrate your report. (Compare 3.2, 3.8)

g) A report on the progress of a journey that you made, or of a historically famous journey, or of an imaginary journey. If helpful, include a drawing to illustrate your report. (Compare 3.8)

h) A report on a book you recently read. (Compare 3.9)

i) A report on problems you had with something you just bought or rented, such as an appliance or a vacation house.

j) A report on a meeting of an organization you belong to.

4 Articles

The following sentences form an article, but they are in the wrong order. Put them in logical order. Discuss how the underlined words and phrases help you. Then compare your answers with those of others. You may want to write out the article, dividing it into three paragraphs.

Ancient Mayan Tomb Discovered

a) 7   Scientists hoped that <u>the last item</u>, <u>the male skeleton</u>, would help them determine whose tomb it was and how Mayans of that era lived.

b) 1   In the thickly grown remote jungles of northern Guatemala at Rio Azul in May of 1984, archeologists located an ancient painted Mayan tomb.

c) 8   In short, archeologists hope that the new tomb at Rio Azul will be as fruitful and significant for the study of the Mayans as <u>Pacal's tomb at Palenque</u>.

d) 3   Archeologists explained that a great deal was learned about the Mayans from <u>another similar tomb</u>, found in 1952 in Palenque, Mexico, which <u>also contained a skeleton</u>, that of Pacal.

e)   Included in the contents of <u>the newly discovered 1,500-year-old tomb</u> were elaborate wall paintings, pottery, and a male skeleton.

f) 4   By deciphering the inscriptions on <u>Pacal's stone coffin, or sarcophagus</u>, archeologists figured out that this ruler was born in the year 603 and died in 683.

g) 2   <u>The tomb</u> was thought to be more than 1,500 years old and, much to the satisfaction of <u>the archeologists</u>, had never been touched by looters.

h) 5   In addition to <u>the sarcophagus inscrip-</u>

Archeologist Richard Adamas visits the 1,500-year-old Mayan tomb in Rio Azul.

tions, <u>these archeologists</u> used pictographs found in the tomb of Pacal to help them understand Mayan hieroglyphics and Mayan history.

33

4.2   *RELATING IDEAS: LINKING WORDS AND PHRASES*

Below is an article on nuclear hazards. Notice the linking words and phrases underlined in paragraph 1. In your group, discuss what they mean, how they link ideas, and how they are punctuated. Then choose the best word or phrase for each blank from the list below the article.

Hazards from Nuclear Power

There are three separate sources of hazard in the process of supplying energy by nuclear power.

(1) First, the radioactive material must travel from its place of manufacture to the power station. (2) Although the power stations themselves are solidly built, the containers used for the transport of the materials are not. There are normally only two methods of transport available, (3) namely road or rail. Unfortunately, both of these involve close contact with the general public, (4) since the routes are sure to pass near, or even through, heavily populated areas.

(5) _____, there is the problem of waste. All nuclear power stations produce wastes that in most cases will remain radioactive for thousands of years. It is impossible to make these wastes nonradioactive, and (6) _____ they must be stored in one of the inconvenient ways that scientists have invented. (7) _____, they may be buried under the

ground, or dropped into abandoned mines, or sunk in the sea. (8) _____, these methods do not solve the problem, (9) _____ an earthquake could easily crack the containers open.

(10) _____, there is the problem of accidental exposure due to a leak or an explosion at the power station. As with the other

two hazards, this is not very likely, (11) _____ it does not provide a serious objection to the nuclear program. (12) _____, it can happen.

Separately, these three types of risks are not a great cause for concern. Taken together, (13) _____, the probability of disaster is extremely high.

Choices:

5. a) second   b) third   c) in that case
6. a) because   b) so   c) after
7. a) besides   b) for example   c) after all
8. a) by the way   b) lastly   c) however
9. a) though   b) since   c) after
10. a) third   b) for instance   c) in conclusion
11. a) so   b) instead   c) namely
12. a) although   b) nevertheless   c)therefore
13. a) although   b) though   c) even though

4.3   *WRITING FIRST AND LAST PARAGRAPHS*

In the following article the first and last paragraphs are missing. After the article there are three alternatives for each. Working in groups, decide which is the best first and last paragraph and discuss why.

(*First paragraph missing*)

The police say hundreds of offenders have been caught by Mrs. Gordon, a citizen who writes down the license numbers of people who break the law in this way, and sends them in to the local police station.

"Anyone can sign a ticket," said a police officer, "and she's signed a lot."

A driver was heading down Clifton Avenue this morning, when she found herself stopped behind a school bus with its red lights flashing. Instead of stopping, the driver started to overtake the bus. But Mrs. Gordon was on the spot, and warned her not to do it. However, the driver passed the bus anyway, and Mrs. Gordon wrote down her license number.

Another driver received a summons in the mail after a similar incident a few weeks ago. When she entered the courtroom, she found Mrs. Gordon there, notebook in hand. "They tell me I should be a policewoman, but I don't want to be," says Mrs. Gordon. "It's just that these people are breaking the law, and they shouldn't. I don't like to see drivers breaking the law when children's lives are involved."

Every weekday morning Mrs. Gordon stands in front of the main supermarket in town, notebook and pencil ready, waiting to catch people passing school buses illegally. "Nobody else wants to be bothered," she says, "but I won't just sit there twiddling my thumbs. I want to do something about it." She began her personal campaign a year ago when her 13-year-old son Jack started taking the school bus.

(*Last paragraph missing*)

Choices for first paragraph:

a) According to the law in New Merton, it is an offense for any driver to overtake a school bus when it has stopped with its red lights flashing. This law is intended to reduce the number of accidents caused by children running across the road when they get off the bus. There are many traffic laws that Margaret Gordon supports.

b) Margaret Gordon is a one-woman police force when it comes to motorists who illegally pass stopped buses. Thanks to her personal campaign, parts of New Merton have become safer for children. She takes down the number of any offender and sends it to the police. But her job is not an easy one.

c) Margaret Gordon doesn't drive a car. She doesn't like publicity, and she doesn't like telling the police about people, but she often writes to the police, and the police sometimes take action. She hates traffic because the school buses stop, but the cars don't, so many motorists hate her.

⟫→

Choices for last paragraph:

a)   Mrs. Gordon wears very nice clothes, and she is a pretty woman. I think it's a pity she has to do this all the time, don't you? I mean, it would be better if people obeyed the laws and stopped behind the buses, but they don't. What do you think? Do you always stop when you see a school bus? I don't, I must admit, but I'm going to make a special effort to do so in the future. Why don't you?

b)   In summary, Mrs. Gordon has made a lot of money for New Merton. Of the 57 tickets she has written, 39 have resulted in the payment of fines totaling over $400. Since there are about 80 school buses in operation, this means an average of about $5 per ticket. Money is important to Mrs. Gordon.

c)   Mrs. Gordon declined to be photographed. She said she didn't want any motorists taking action in revenge. "I don't particularly want people to pay fines," she says. "It's not that I like writing out tickets. I just want people to obey the law, that's all."

4.4   SELECTING AND ORDERING INFORMATION

You have been asked to write a feature article for a local newspaper on shopping by computer. Below is the beginning of the article. Working in a group, decide which other points to include and why. Then group the points into paragraphs, and, individually, write each paragraph adding suitable linking words, phrases, and/or sentences where necessary to relate the ideas. Finally, write a conclusion.

Shopping by Computer

It's not enough that the computer is invading our work and play worlds. It has started to invade our shopping world as well. Shopping by computer, or teleshopping, is a phenomenon that is beginning to appear in homes, stores, hotels, and even airports. The service allows the shopper to look at electronic catalogs and to order items, such as dishes or clothing or concert tickets, without leaving the computer.

Select from these points:

Teleshopping is convenient for people, especially those who don't live near large cities.

Owners of teleshopping services hope that people will find shopping by computer more convenient than fighting crowds and traffic in shopping centers and stores.

One user reports that it is much more fun than going out to shop.

Only a small number of households own a computer.

It is still very difficult to put a picture of an item on a computer screen. —

Shopping by computer will hurt store sales. —

Prices for items bought through a computer can be lower than store prices because of lower overhead costs○

The teleshopping business is still young.○

The easiest items to sell through computer today are such things as tickets and well-known appliances that do not need salespeople and pictures. —

Computers are only for the wealthy. —

I can shop by computer at midnight if I want to without worrying about stores being closed.○

There is a charge for belonging to such a teleshopping service, for example, $25 per year. —

There are at least five such services in operation right now, and many more are predicted in the years to come. ○

You can buy the same items at home as you can in stores.○

People will always want to shop in person, so computer shopping will not damage store sales. ○

Computer shopping is nothing more than a new video game, and an expensive one at that. —

Stores work hard to make shopping convenient and pleasant for customers. —

Many experts say that this kind of shopping will not become popular until 1995.

Computers are easy and fun to use. ○

4.5   **WRITING AN ARTICLE BASED ON A CONVERSATION**

Below is an interview with a Japanese businessman who has just returned from two years of work in the United States. After reading the interview, write an article on some of the differences between the cultures of Japan and the United States as shown in the interview. Imagine you are writing for the corporation's newspaper in Japan.

Interviewer:	Mr. Kawashima, I understand you have just spent two years working as a manager for a corporation in the United States. Can you tell me something about your experience? What were some of the things that surprised you about life there – let's say with social life?
Mr. Kawashima:	One thing that surprised me a great deal was that people who work together don't socialize on weekends as we do in Japan, for example, playing golf on Saturdays. They'll have occasional get-togethers like a barbecue or dinner . . . but then the whole family is invited.
Interviewer:	Yes, it's true, in Japan the family is rarely invited to a business affair. Did you get used to that?
Mr. Kawashima:	Well, I did, but one embarrassing thing happened the first time my boss invited me and my family to a barbecue at his home. Because it was a party at my boss's house, I wore business clothes – suit, shirt, and tie. When I got there, I discovered that all the other men were wearing shorts or blue jeans! I'm afraid I added to a Japanese stereotype, that we never take off our "uniforms." My wife had a hard time at first, too, with these kinds of parties. You know, she wasn't used to socializing with the wives of my colleagues. She rarely, if ever, did that in Japan. But now she likes and expects to be included. She'll have a hard time getting used to the Japanese way again, I'm afraid!
Interviewer:	Is there anything else that was different for your family?
Mr. Kawashima:	Yes. In Japan, my wife was not used to having me home at dinnertime every night because, as you know, in Japan many men work late and then have a drink out with colleagues. That didn't happen often where I worked in the United States, so my wife had to adjust to my being home at six-thirty every night instead of nine-thirty or ten o'clock, as in Japan.
Interviewer:	What about your work situation? What was different there?
Mr. Kawashima:	Well, I was impressed with the way business people in the United States make demands, like asking for a raise or a promotion. We would never think of doing that so directly in Japan.
Interviewer:	Do people always get what they ask for in the United States?
Mr. Kawashima:	No, of course not. But they do tend to take more initiative in their professional careers. In fact, I was amazed that people who are high up in a company sometimes switch to a rival company or even to a company in a completely different line of work!
Interviewer:	And in Japan, people usually stay with the same company all of their lives. How does that compare with the United States?
Mr. Kawashima:	It's hard to say. But it seems to me that people in the United

States are more likely to change companies quite often in order to get a raise or a promotion. In fact, in the United States, I've met only one or two people who have been at the same company their whole lives.

Interviewer: Is there anything else that struck you during your time there?

Mr. Kawashima: I could add one thing about personal relations on the job. As you know, in Japan, if you have a personal problem, you often talk it over with your boss. In contrast, people in the United States don't do that much. Oh yes, my colleagues in the U.S. also kept photos of their families on their desks!

Interviewer: Well, these are interesting differences! Thank you, Mr. Kawashima. I'm sure our readers will find this very informative.

Before writing your article, you may want to organize what you are going to say. Outlining the major points made in the interview may help. An outline is started for you:

Some differences between the cultures of Japan and the United States:
1. Social life
   - Japan: frequent weekend socializing for businessmen (golf). Family not included.
   - U.S.: occasional weekend socializing (barbecues, dinners). Family included, wife socializes with husband's colleagues.
2. Family life
   - Japan: husband not home at dinnertime.
   - United States: husbands home at 6:30 for dinner
3. Work situation / difference in the way business people make demands

---

4.6   WRITING AN ARTICLE BASED ON VISUAL INFORMATION

ex. asking for a raise or promotion

A. *The following article, with the graph, explains reports of people seeing unidentified flying objects (UFOs). Read it; then, working in groups, underline the words and phrases in the article that refer specifically to the different parts of the graph.*

Unidentified Flying Objects (UFOs)

During the early part of January of this year the rate of UFO reports was steady, around three or four per week. When, however, on Monday, January 16, a science fiction film about visitors from outer space was shown on television, there was an immediate sharp increase in reports of sightings from all parts of the state. The commanding officer of Tawukee Air Force Base, General Wayne Tyler, who is directly responsible for the investigation of all such reports, decided to make his findings known. On Monday, January 30, the Iowa *Chronicle* carried an article written by Tyler, which maintained that all UFO reports could be explained quite naturally by civil and military aircraft movements. Following this explanation, there was a rapid drop in the number of reported sightings, although the rate remained above the pre-broadcast level.

Some people were not convinced by the article. One skeptic was Martin Hogarty, science correspondent of the city newspaper. On Friday, February 17, Hogarty published a highly critical piece about the air force, claiming that they were trying to cover up evidence about UFOs, and demanding an independent inquiry. This article caused a renewed interest in the subject of UFOs and a steep rise in the number of reported sightings, although not as steep as the increase in

⟫→

January.

General Tyler at once invited Hogarty to meet him in a public debate ten days later. The TV station agreed to air the debate. Inexplicably, Hogarty did not show up for the debate, and the commander was able to produce some very convincing evidence for his case.

As a result, interest in UFOs fell to rock bottom: Sightings were even lower than at the beginning of the year. As the weeks went by, there was a slight increase in the number of reports, but this only brought the rate back to the normal level of three or four per week, where it has remained ever since.

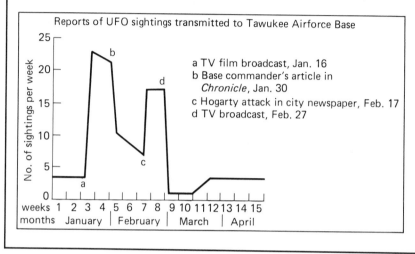

Reports of UFO sightings transmitted to Tawukee Airforce Base

a TV film broadcast, Jan. 16
b Base commander's article in *Chronicle*, Jan. 30
c Hogarty attack in city newspaper, Feb. 17
d TV broadcast, Feb. 27

B. *Now, either alone or in groups, write an article to go along with the graph and information below on immigration to the United States, 1820–1980.*

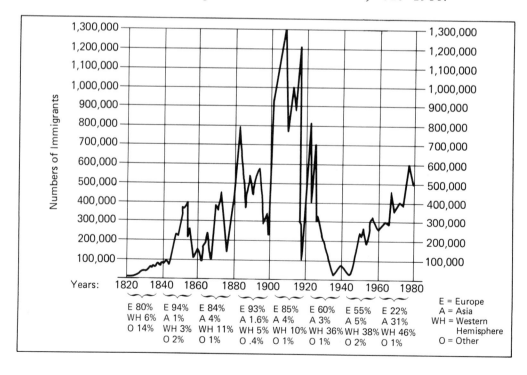

1820–40:   After 1750, European population doubled; Industrial Revolution
             caused much unemployment; Westward expansion continued in U.S.
1840–60:   Irish potato famine 1845–49; ocean travel became safer; Germans and
             Scandinavians took up farming in Midwest; 1850, California Gold
             Rush
1860–80:   Chinese workers went to West, mostly to build railroads
1880–1900:   1882 Chinese Exclusion Act limited Chinese immigration; many
             Italians, Czechs, Poles, and Jews immigrated
1900–20:   1907 was year of highest immigration; 1917 Immigration Act excluded
             Asians, required literacy
1920–40:   1924 National Origins Act established quotas for each country outside
             Western Hemisphere; 1929–35 Stock Market Crash and Great
             Depression reduced numbers of immigrants
1940–60:   World War II; starting 1948, war refugees admitted
1960–80:   Various refugee acts allowed refugees admission; 1965 Immigration Act
             opened more immigration from Third World

4.7   ADDING EXAMPLES AND DETAILS

*Below is an incomplete article on communicative styles. Notice that it introduces a
topic and makes some statements about different kinds of communicative styles.
However, it does not give many details or any examples about each style. Working in
groups, add details and examples to each paragraph. Use the chart following the
article to help you.*

Communicative Styles

Many executives are discovering that personality
clashes are affecting their business. Consequently,
they are hiring experts to analyze the communicative
styles of their personnel. One such expert is Dr. Paul
Mok, a psychological consultant in Dallas, Texas. Dr.
Mok maintains that relating to the style of the people
you deal with helps you communicate effectively in
the business world. If two styles clash, business deals
suffer. He outlines four basic communicative styles,
each with different characteristics.

The Intuitor is an "idea" person, a problem solver,
a person who likes theories and looks to the future.

_____

_____

_____

_____

The Thinker is objective; he or she likes logic,

⟫→

ideas, and systematic inquiry. _____

_____

_____

_____

_____

The Feeler is warm, perceptive, and personable; he or she works well with human emotions. _____

_____

_____

_____

The Sensor is a doer, one who emphasizes action and getting things done. _____

_____

_____

_____

Dr. Mok believes that recognizing your own style and adjusting it to that of the person across the desk from you can help you conduct business successfully.

CHARACTERISTICS OF EACH COMMUNICATIVE STYLE

	Intuitor	*Thinker*	*Feeler*	*Sensor*
Speech:	Wordy, impersonal	Businesslike, specific	Friendly, humorous	Abrupt, direct
Writing:	Intellectual	Well-organized	Personal	Brief
Clothing:	Mixed, unpredictable	Conservative	Colorful, informal	Informal, simple
Most likely profession:	Lawyer, engineer, scientist, accountant	Scientist, researcher	Entertainer, teacher, nurse	Executive, salesperson, manager

4.8   *PUNCTUATING:* COMMAS, PERIODS, AND SEMICOLONS

Compare these three ways of punctuating the same information:

1. Many people find large supermarkets convenient places for buying their groceries. Others prefer the intimacy of small grocery stores.
2. Many people find large supermarkets convenient places for buying their groceries, but others prefer the intimacy of small grocery stores.
3. Many people find large supermarkets convenient places for buying their groceries; others prefer the intimacy of small grocery stores.

Working in groups, discuss why sentence 2 uses a comma rather than a period or a semicolon. Would a comma be correct in sentences 1 and 3? Why or why not? The

⟫→

Super marketing

You can still buy a can of string beans or a box of cereal at the USA's supermarkets, but you also can have lunch, get a haircut, mail a letter and send flowers to a favorite aunt at many of them. Here are some of the new services available:

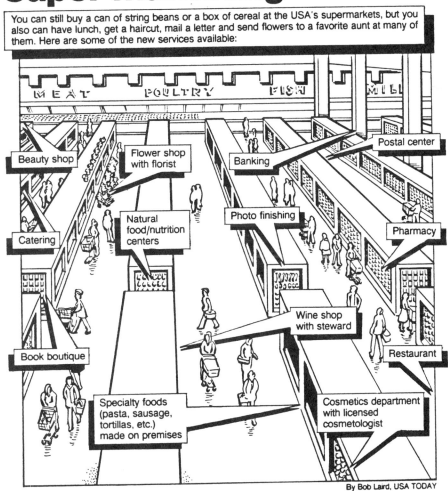

MEAT   POULTRY   FISH   MILK

Beauty shop

Flower shop with florist

Banking

Postal center

Natural food/nutrition centers

Photo finishing

Pharmacy

Catering

Book boutique

Wine shop with steward

Restaurant

Specialty foods (pasta, sausage, tortillas, etc.) made on premises

Cosmetics department with licensed cosmetologist

By Bob Laird, USA TODAY

following sentences need some changes in punctuation to make them correct. Correct the punctuation and add any connecting words you wish.

4. The modern supermarket is very different from the small grocery store of yesterday, it's bigger, it offers a greater variety of services.
5. Shoppers in today's supermarkets don't have a lot of time to spend shopping, they look for convenience and efficiency.
6. Managers of supermarkets cater to this, they offer many convenience foods, they try not to sacrifice freshness or quality.
7. Managers also recognize their customers' desire for relaxation, they pipe in calming music, they use soft colors for decorating.
8. You can do many things besides shop for food in today's supermarket, you can purchase prescriptions from the pharmacy section, you can get your hair cut at the beauty shop, you might do your banking in the banking area.
9. Today's shoppers enjoy the convenience of modern supermarkets, they also miss the uniqueness of small grocery stores.

4.9   PRACTICING WRITING ARTICLES

Choose one of the following topics. Write:

a) A newspaper article about a recent discovery or invention. (Compare 4.1)
b) An article on other sources of energy, such as coal, oil, solar, wind, gas, and others, and their problems. (Compare 4.2)
c) An article on a type of pollution, such as air pollution, noise pollution, or water pollution. (Compare 4.2)
d) A feature article about someone who does something different in spite of what others think. (Compare 4.3)
e) An article on a social phenomenon, such as computer banking or electronic music. (Compare 4.4 and 4.8)
f) An article showing some differences between the culture of your country and that of the United States (or some other country). (Compare 4.5) You may wish to interview someone who has just returned from the United States or someone who knows a lot about both countries or a classmate from another country.
g) An article that describes and contrasts two or more different groups or types of people. (Compare 4.7)
h) A short article on the advantages and disadvantages of:
records compared with cassette tapes
supermarkets compared with small shops
private enterprise compared with public enterprise
two different modes of transportation
i) An article about recent changes in the roles of men and women in your country.
j) An article on recent scientific research, for example in the fields of health and medicine.

5 Instructions

5.1   ***ORGANIZING IDEAS***

The following sentences are a set of instructions, but they are in the wrong order. Working in a group, put them in logical order. Discuss how the underlined words help you. When you have finished, write the instructions out in the form of a paragraph.

a)   <u>Next</u>, push up the switch on the back of the computer to turn on the computer. The POWER light on the keyboard will light up in a few seconds.

b)   <u>Once the disk is in</u>, close the disk drive door.

c)   <u>After the POWER light comes on</u>, press the RESET key in the upper right corner of the keyboard.

d)   <u>To start with</u>, turn on the display screen (monitor).

e)   <u>Finally</u>, press the RETURN key; after a few seconds, a message on the display screen will indicate that the computer is ready to operate.

f)   <u>Once the disk drive door is open</u>, the disk drive is ready to receive the operating disk.

g)   <u>After pressing the RESET key</u>, wait until the red light on the disk drive goes off, and then open the disk drive door.

h)   <u>Now</u>, remove <u>the disk</u> from its envelope, hold the disk with the label up, and gently slip the disk into the disk drive.

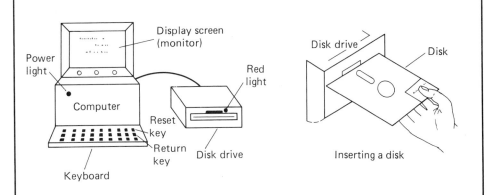

5.2   USING REPORTING WORDS

Compare these two ways of reporting what someone said:

"It's dangerous to cross a city street anywhere, but it's particularly dangerous in Rome," says Luigi to tourists in Rome.
a) Luigi warns tourists about the dangers of crossing a street in Rome.
b) Luigi tells tourists that it's dangerous to cross a city street anywhere, but it's particularly dangerous in Rome.

Notice that in (a) the word WARNS gives an idea of what Luigi said and how he said it without using all of his words.

The following sentences are given in the form of direct speech. Report what this person said. Change each sentence into reported speech. Choose one of the words given after each sentence. You do not need to include every word the person said. The first sentence is done as an example.

1. "First, make sure drivers of oncoming cars see you," Luigi tells tourists, "but don't let them know you see them." (advise/allow/beg)
   Luigi advises tourists to make sure drivers of oncoming cars see them, but not to let them know the tourists see them.
2. "If drivers know pedestrians see them, they'll just blow their horns and race through the intersection," he says. (order/explain/suggest)

3. "Of course, it's always a good idea to look for others who want to cross the street at the same time," Luigi says, "since there's safety in numbers." (order/encourage/warn)
4. "As I've told you before, be careful even with a green light because cars don't always stop for a red light," he says. (urge/remind/admit)
5. "And one more thing. Please, please don't ever hold your hand up like traffic police trying to stop cars," says Luigi. "That technique is for the inexperienced." (suggest/beg/allow)
6. "The best way is to just take a deep breath, say a prayer, and walk across resolutely with eyes straight ahead," says Luigi. (warn/urge/order)

Now choose two or three of the reporting words above and write your own examples of direct and reported speech.

Example:
"Be careful so you do a good job. I know you can," said Mr. Iannelli to his assistant. Mr. Iannelli *encouraged* his assistant to do a good job.

5.3   WRITING PARAGRAPHS

A. *Below is an explanation of how to get a driver's license. As you read the instructions, circle the words that tell the ORDER of the steps.*

First, get a booklet describing the traffic laws and regulations in your area and study the booklet. Next, when you feel you know the driving laws, go to your nearest Motor Vehicles office for a test on the rules of the road. Before you take the test, you'll fill out an application form and pay a fee. If you pass the test, you'll get a learner's permit. Now you can practice driving, but only in the company of a licensed driver. Meanwhile, don't forget the traffic laws you learned so well. Finally, when you can drive well, take the driving test at the Motor Vehicles office. If you pass, you'll get a driver's license. If you don't, practice more and take the test again.

B. *Now write a paragraph of instructions for one of the situations described below. Be sure to use some ORDER words. You may wish to use a diagram.*

1. A visitor wants to make a long-distance call but does not know your city's phone system.
2. A visitor wants to send a telegram but does not know how.
3. A friend is using your apartment or house and needs to know how to work the stove (or other appliance, such as washing machine or hot-water heater.)
4. You need to leave a message for the baby-sitter about how to do a particular task, such as giving the baby a bath or preparing the baby's formula.
5. You need to tell friends how to use a piece of equipment they are borrowing, such as:
   camera – how to load the film
   clock – how to set the alarm
   videocassette recorder – how to record a TV program

5.4   *COMPARING TEXTS: ORGANIZATION*

A. Below are two versions of the same letter. Discuss what kinds of changes were made in the original letter and why the revised letter is better.

Original letter

Dear Maria,

    I'm delighted you'll be working for me again this summer! I know my photography business will be in good hands until I get back next week. Let me go over your schedule and duties. Hours are 9 a.m. to 5 p.m. ¶3 Of course, you'll be answering the phone. Please take messages, and I'll return the calls when I get back. ¶4 Any mail that comes in can be opened. If someone wants an appointment to be photographed, you can make it for the week after next. ~~I should mention that~~ you'll find ~~my~~ *the* ~~appointment~~ book in the top right-hand drawer of the desk. ¶2 The first thing you'll ~~should~~ do in the morning is check the appointment book. There are a few people scheduled to see prints. ~~By the way, another thing to do when opening mail is to see~~ if there are any bills to be paid. Put those in my "bills" box on the desk so I can take care of them when I return. There shouldn't be any urgent bills this week. ¶5 It's a great relief to know someone is taking care of things while I'm gone. ~~One more thing,~~ prints are filed under the customer's name in the brown file cabinet. You've handled this before, so you know the procedure.

    If there's anything you have a question about, my phone number is on the bulletin board. [I'll be working during the day, so it's best to get me at night. I'm on a tough assignment, so not too late, please!]

As always,

Lee

Handwritten margin notes:
- 2nd sentence in ¶2
- end of ¶ 4
- end of ¶ 2
- Night is the best time to get me, but not too late, please!

Revised letter

Dear Maria,

    I'm delighted you'll be working for me again this summer! I know my photography business will be in good hands until I get back next week. Let me go over your schedule and duties. Hours are from 9 a.m. to 5 p.m.

    The first thing you'll do in the morning is check the appointment book. You'll find the book in the top right-hand drawer of the desk. There are a few people scheduled to see prints. Prints are filed under the customer's name in the brown file cabinet. You've handled this before, so you know the procedure.

    Of course, you'll be answering the phone. Please take messages, and I'll return the calls when I get back.

    Any mail that comes in can be opened. If someone wants an appointment to be photographed, you can make it for the week after next. If there are bills to be paid, put them in the "bills" box on the desk so I can take care of them when I return.

    It's a great relief to know someone is taking care of things while I'm gone. If there's anything you have a question about, my phone number is on the bulletin board. Night is the best time to get me, but not too late, please!

As always,

Lee

B. *Discuss what changes would make the letter below better. Then rewrite the letter, making the necessary revisions and deleting unimportant information. It may help you to outline or list the main points (as you did in 4.5) before you start.*

apt. 43
1501 19th N.E.
Seattle, Washington 98063
June 10, 1990

Dear Lillian and George,

We're happy that you're going to be subletting our apartment for the month of July. Anita has told us a lot about you, so we feel we almost know you. As requested, here are a few instructions.

You can pick up the keys from our downstairs neighbor, Jan, but you'd better call her first to make sure she'll be in (665-3031). She works during the day and often goes out at night. Anyway, there are five keys, three for the apartment door and two for the main door. In fact, if you need help with anything, you can always ask Jan, or Ron, who lives next door. I think he's unemployed now, so he's home during the day. By the way, use any of the kitchen utensils and bedding you want.

The only responsibility you'll have is taking the mail out of the mailbox every day. Oh, and please water the plants every four or five days. The mailbox key is hanging on a nail on the back of the door. I should mention the terrace, too. Feel free to use it for sitting, sunbathing, or whatever. Just be sure to lock the porch door when you finish. By the way, the bedding and towels are on a shelf in the bathroom. When you water the plants, please don't forget those on the porch. In fact, those should be watered almost every day unless it rains. Incidentally, return the keys to Jan when you leave. If there are any phone calls for us, you can tell people that we'll be back August 1. Our number is 218-936-1127. You may want our number in case you need to contact us. Our landlord can be reached at 536-1819 if you have trouble with plumbing, refrigerator, or electricity. That's about everything, I think. Enjoy your stay!

Sincerely,
Henry Knorr

5.5   *WRITING TEXT BASED ON VISUAL INFORMATION*

A. *Look at the map below. Then read the instructions on how to get from Tartu College to five places for shopping in downtown Toronto, Canada.*

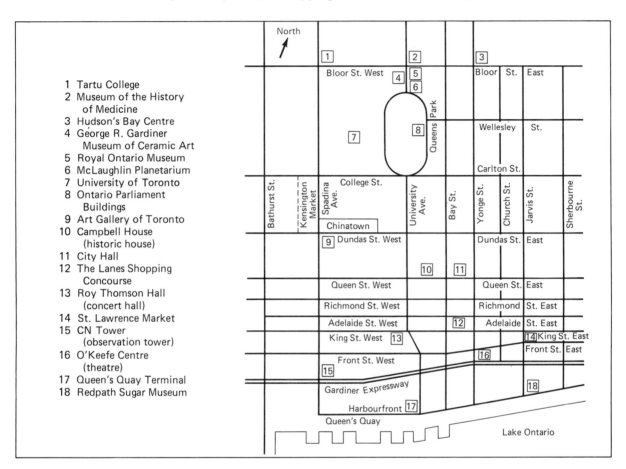

1 Tartu College
2 Museum of the History
   of Medicine
3 Hudson's Bay Centre
4 George R. Gardiner
   Museum of Ceramic Art
5 Royal Ontario Museum
6 McLaughlin Planetarium
7 University of Toronto
8 Ontario Parliament
   Buildings
9 Art Gallery of Toronto
10 Campbell House
   (historic house)
11 City Hall
12 The Lanes Shopping
   Concourse
13 Roy Thomson Hall
   (concert hall)
14 St. Lawrence Market
15 CN Tower
   (observation tower)
16 O'Keefe Centre
   (theatre)
17 Queen's Quay Terminal
18 Redpath Sugar Museum

1. You may want to drive, as it's quite far to walk. Start on Bloor Street West and go east to the corner of Bloor and Yonge Streets. Hudson's Bay Centre, a big shopping complex, is on the corner.
2. From Hudson's Bay, go south on Yonge Street until you get to Adelaide Street. Turn right at the corner of Yonge and Adelaide Streets and go half a block west on Adelaide Street. There'll find the entrance to the Lanes Shopping Concourse, which is underground. You should be able to park on Adelaide Street.
3. From there, go two and a half blocks east on Adelaide Street to Jarvis Street. Turn right on Jarvis and go two blocks south. You'll find the St. Lawrence Market, a large food market, at the corner of Jarvis and Front Street East.
4. Queen's Quay Terminal is a shopping complex in Harbourfront. To get there from St. Lawrence Market, go south two blocks to Queen's Quay. Turn right and go three long blocks to University Avenue. The Terminal is on your right.
5. On your way back to Tartu College, you can stop at two more areas for shopping, Chinatown and Kensington Market. Go west on Queen's Quay to Spadina Avenue. Turn right and go about seven blocks north to Dundas Street

West. Chinatown is to your right along Dundas Street West, and Kensington Market is on Spadina Avenue between Dundas Street West and College Street.

B. *Someone staying at Tartu College wants to see the sights in Toronto. Pick at least five places for the visitor to see and write the directions.*

5.6   *WRITING TEXT BASED ON A CONVERSATION*

Below is a conversation you overhear between two friends, one of whom started her own business and has been successful with it. After reading the conversation, write a short piece that gives people advice or instructions on how to start their own business. It may help you to outline or list the important points (as you did in 4.5) before you start writing.

Y: Well, it's Elizabeth Chin! I haven't seen you for months! What've you been up to?

E: Oh, I've been really busy with my new business. It takes an awful lot of time, especially at the beginning – picking people's brains at lunch or dinner; working over lunch with my employees; getting experts in marketing, exporting, and finance to be on my board of directors; making up careful budgets; reading everything I can get my hands on about the import/export field . . .

Y: Well, has all this time and work paid off?

E: You bet. It's been well worth all the energy. My business is beginning to take off!

Y: Congratulations! What else did you do to get such a good start?

E: Well, for one thing, I hired smart people! I've learned a lot from them. I try hard to listen to their advice – and I've encouraged them to continue to grow professionally by attending seminars and development courses.

Y: What about your own training? Anything new for you?

E: Yes, I've been taking courses in business administration weekends and evenings. The courses have taught me a lot, and the contacts I've made have been invaluable. In fact, I hired one of my classmates as a consultant to help us solve a particular problem, and I got another classmate to conduct a weekly seminar on new marketing techniques.

Y: Gee, I've been thinking of getting into the landscaping business. Any suggestions?

E: Well, first make sure you really want to do it, because it'll be your whole life for the first few years, at least! And you should make sure no one else is doing exactly the same thing in your area – that is, check out the competition. Then, thorough market research is essential – to find out how much call there is for landscaping around here, who your customers will be, and what kind of services they want. I've learned a lot from my customers and potential customers, as well as from my suppliers. Planning is also important – you need to figure out how much money you'll need to get started, right down to the last paper clip!

Y: Sounds like a lot of work.

E: You said it – it took me a year of research and planning before I was ready to get started.

Y: I'm so glad I ran into you! Can we have lunch next week so I can pick your brains even more?

E: Of course! I'm flattered to be asked!

5.7   *PUNCTUATING: COMMAS AND PERIODS*

A. *In the following recipe, notice the use of commas and periods, especially those with abbreviations. Discuss with others why commas could not be used in place of periods.*

PARSLEYED RICE

3 c. water   ¼ c. butter cut into 6 pieces
1½ c. uncooked rice   1 c. chopped parsley
1 tsp. salt

   Bring the water to a boil in a heavy pan. Stir in the rice and salt. Once the water is boiling again, reduce heat to low and cover tightly. Let the rice cook, without stirring, for 25 minutes. Uncover the pan. Add the butter and parsley, without stirring, and cover the pan. Remove the pan from heat and let stand. After 5 minutes, uncover the pan, toss rice with a fork to mix in the butter and parsley, and serve with Spanish-Style Chicken.

B. *Now, working individually, put commas, periods, and capital letters in the following recipe.*

SPANISH-STYLE CHICKEN

1 chicken cut into pieces   1½ c chopped green or
½ tsp salt   red peppers
¼ tsp black pepper   ⅓ c dry white wine or
1 T butter   water
1 T oil   2 c diced tomatoes
½ c chopped onion   1 bay leaf
1 tsp finely minced garlic

   salt and pepper the chicken pieces and set them aside heat butter and oil in a large heavy skillet add chicken putting skin-side down and cook over medium-high heat 5 minutes turn and continue cooking about 5 minutes turning occasionally when chicken pieces are brown add onion garlic peppers and wine or water cook about 10 minutes stirring and then add tomatoes and bay leaf cover and let cook 20 minutes uncover and cook 10 minutes longer

---

5.8   PRACTICING WRITING INSTRUCTIONS

Choose one of the following topics. Write:

a) Instructions, with a diagram, for how to operate a machine that you know well, such as a record player. (Compare 5.1 and 5.3)

b) Instructions for someone who needs to know how to apply for a passport, how to apply for a scholarship, or how to insert a contact lens. (Compare 5.3)

c) Instructions for someone who is going to use your house or apartment while you are away, or look after your garden, or care for your child. Take into account different circumstances that might arise. (Compare 5.4)

d) Instructions, with a map, to tell someone how to get from one place to another. (Compare 5.5)

e) Instructions telling someone how to do something, such as give a speech, or organize your time efficiently, or study for a particular exam. (Compare 5.6)

f) One of your favorite recipes to be published in a community cookbook. (Compare 5.7)

g) Instructions for someone who wants to learn how to play a simple game you know.

h) Instructions for someone who is going to do a small job for you, either in your home or at your job.

6 Business letters and memos

ORGANIZING IDEAS

The following sentences form a complete memo, but they are in the wrong order. Working in groups, put them in the right order. Discuss how the underlined words and phrases help link the memo together. Then write out the memo, dividing it into three paragraphs.

MEMORANDUM

To: All Staff

From: Pierre Aries   August 3

---

a) I am sure, <u>therefore</u>, that all of you will join with me in sending condolences to her husband and family.

b) She was <u>equally appreciated</u> by people outside the company for her active participation in community groups, especially the Public Library Volunteers and Literacy Volunteers.

c) Unfortunately, <u>this was unsuccessful</u>, and she died in her sleep the next day.

d) As many of you know, <u>she had been ill for some time</u>, and on Tuesday underwent emergency surgery.

e) <u>Only a few days before this</u>, she had been in contact with office personnel by phone, still very concerned about the new health benefit plan that she initiated last year.

f) Anyone with a personal family problem, <u>for example</u>, could always count on her sympathy and support.

g) It is with deep regret that I announce the death of our office manager, Ms. Margaret Len.

h) Within the firm, <u>on the other</u> hand, she will be best remembered for her loyalty to, and her concern for, all members of the staff.

i) <u>The health plan</u> was a typical product of Ms. Len's interest in employees' well-being, and it made her much appreciated by all employees.

6.2   *RELATING IDEAS: LINKING WORDS AND PHRASES*

Below is an office memo. Notice the underlined linking words and phrases at the beginning of the memo. In your group, discuss what they mean, how they link ideas, and how they are punctuated.

Then choose the best word or phrase for each blank from the list below the memo.

OFFICE MEMORANDUM

To: Director   Date: Sept. 3
From: Office Manager   Subject: Reducing Staff

I have several proposals for cutting down on office staff. (1) <u>First</u>, I suggest that we eliminate the full-time position of order clerk, (2) <u>since</u> there is not enough work to occupy him throughout the month. Orders and requests for sales information are heaviest at the end of the month; (3) <u>in contrast</u>, there is little to do the first two weeks of each month. (4) <u>Therefore</u>, I recommend that we hire temporary help for the last two weeks of each month and give the orders from the first of the month to the sales department to process.

(5) _____, now that our systems are completely computerized we no longer need a computer programmer on staff. It's true, we will need computer programming services occasionally in future, (6) _____, when we revise our billing system. In such cases, (7) _____, we can hire a freelance programmer.

(8) _____, I suggest that I share my secretary with the assistant office manager, (9) _____ eliminating one secretarial position. (10) _____ this will increase the managerial workload, I feel we can handle it. (11) _____, we can always hire temporary help to get us through particularly busy periods.

If these suggestions are followed, we should be able to save approximately $26,000 in the coming year in salaries alone. (12) _____, I believe these changes will result in greater work efficiency.

Choose from these:

5. a) second   b) in contrast   c) otherwise
6. a) consequently   b) for instance   c) even though
7. a) however   b) in addition   c) second
8. a) third   b) however   c) after all
9. a) in contrast   b) likewise   c) thus
10. a) although   b) since   c) so
11. a) finally   b) consequently   c) moreover
12. a) while   b) so   c) in addition

6.3 USING REPORTING WORDS

Compare these two ways of reporting what someone said. Working in groups, discuss the use of the words ADMIT and PROMISE.

"O.K., we made a small mistake in the calculations," Ms. Aristede said to her assistant, "but they don't have to get so upset about it. Anyway, we'll get the revised figures to them by the end of the week."
a) Ms. Aristede admitted that a small mistake was made, but she promised that the revised figures would arrive by the end of the week.
b) Ms. Aristede said that they had made a small mistake in the calculations, but that they didn't have to get so upset about it. She said that they would get the revised figures to them by the end of the week anyway.

Notice that the words ADMIT and PROMISE say what Ms. Aristede said and how she said it, but with fewer words than appear in example (b).

Report the following snatches of conversation, using one of the three reporting words given after each sentence. You can report each piece of conversation in one sentence or in two sentences, as you wish.

1. "Good morning, Genaro," said the director. (say/greet/offer) "Do you have my mail?" (admit/remind/ask)
   The director greeted Genaro and asked if he had his mail.
2. "In my opinion, what these people say about overcharging is complete nonsense," said the accountant. (think/intend/promise) "What they ought to do is to compare our prices with those of some of our competitors!" (threaten/suggest/ask)
3. "I've told you before, and I'll tell you again," the foreman said to his workers. "There is definitely something wrong with those machines." (promise/offer/insist) Then he added, "You'll risk injury if you use the machines before they've been properly serviced." (warn/tell/urge)
4. "Mr. Johnson," said the director's assistant, "as I've told you before, this is a private area." (announce/remind/offer) "If you don't leave this office at once, I'll have to call security." (threaten/boast/suggest)
5. "I give you my word," said the director, "that I won't tell anyone what you say, Mr. Fong." (ask/greet/promise) "But I strongly suggest you put your comments on paper for the record." (urge/allow/explain)

Now choose two or three of the reporting words above. Write examples of direct speech and reported speech to show their use.

Example:
"I realize now I've done the job all wrong. I plan to do it over again," said Paul.
Paul *admitted* he had done the job wrong. He *intends* (intended) to do it over again.   *or*   Paul admitted he had done the job wrong and intends to do it over again.

6.4   *WRITING FIRST AND LAST PARAGRAPHS*

A. *Following is a memo of three paragraphs. The last paragraph is missing. Working in groups, decide which suggestion makes the best last paragraph. Then discuss your answer and reasons with those of other groups.*

Catco COMPUTERS, INC.

MEMO TO: Directors and all Sales, Finance, and Technical
          Staff
FROM: Alain Nikro

REPORT ON FIFTH ANNUAL INTERNATIONAL COMPUTER EXHIBITION,
HONG KONG, 1-8 APRIL

    The exhibit was extremely successful for us again this year, as it has been in the past. Our new models received an enthusiastic response and orders were high. There were, however, two problems we should address before they begin to adversely affect our business at the exhibition.

    First, the size of our stand at the exhibition was the same as last year's (700 square feet), even though we added three new models to our line. This made our exhibit extremely crowded.

    Second, our exhibit was staffed only with sales representatives. Therefore, when customers - who are becoming increasingly sophisticated - had a technical question, the sales reps were usually unable to answer it.

Choices for fourth paragraph:

a) Therefore, there were several competitors who had stands of 1,000 square feet or more, and even some of the Japanese competitors had stands larger than ours. Since we were all in the same area, it was quite easy to see the effect on potential customers, and it certainly made us think.

⟫→

b) Therefore, I suggest the following. Next year we should increase the size of the stand to 900 square feet in order to accommodate the new models and to give customers sufficient room to examine them. We should also make sure that there is at least one technician at the exhibit at all times, to provide technical information and advice to customers. Please let me know your reactions to these suggestions.

c) It is true, of course, that we have so far maintained a good share of the market and our total sales have in fact risen slightly in each of the last three years. But we cannot simply hope that these things will continue, and we must think of the future.

B. *Following are the second and third paragraphs of a business letter from B. N. Dumont to Lester Duval. Working either alone or in groups, write a suitable first paragraph. Then compare your version with those of others.*

Mr. Lester Duval
Haverfields Business Machines
45 Townsend Street
San Francisco, California 94107

Dear Mr. Duval:

(First paragraph missing)

    First, you do not mention the questions of transport and insurance. Can we assume that you accept responsibility for both of these, and that your quoted price includes the cost? If not, could you let us know how you usually deal with these matters, and what the cost is likely to be?

    Second, we find your letter somewhat vague as to delivery dates. You mention that there may be strikes which are beyond your control. Obviously, strikes are even less within our control. We would like you to accept responsibility at least for any possible strikes in your company.

    We look forward to hearing from you on both these points.

                  Sincerely,

                  B. N. Dumont

                  B. N. Dumont

6.5   *COMPARING TEXTS*

Read each help-wanted ad and letter below.

Working in groups, decide which of the letters is better organized and more appropriately written. Discuss your decision and reasons with other groups. Finally, rewrite the poorly written letter.

HOTEL

CONFERENCE MANAGER

Plan and facilitate all conferences held in hotel. Contact and solicit clients, handle conference contracts, plan work schedules of hotel staff, settle client and staff complaints. Bilingual Spanish/English. Degree preferred. Contact Martha Alvarez, Hotel Del Prado, Juarez 70, Mexico City D.F., Mexico.

Letter 1:

```
                                        300 W. San Mateo Rd.
                                        Santa Fe, New Mexico 07504 USA
                                        July 2, 1990

Ms. Martha Alvarez
Hotel Del Prado
Juarez 70
Mexico City D.F., Mexico

Dear Ms. Alvarez:

     I am writing in response to your advertisement for the position of
Conference Manager (Hotels Today Magazine, July 1, 1990).
     I am currently Assistant Conference Manager at the Sheraton de Santa
Fe Hotel and Conference Center, where I have worked since 1980. My
promotion to this position came after three years as a secretary in the
Conference Manager's office.
     I have had extensive experience in arranging conferences, conferring
with potential clients, and directing hotel personnel. I enjoy all aspects
of conference management and believe I now have the right combination of
experience and training to take on the challenge of Conference Manager.
     I earned my university degree in Hotel Management at the College of
Santa Fe. My educational background, the fact that I grew up in a Spanish-
speaking community in Santa Fe and am therefore bilingual in Spanish and
```

Unit 6   Business letters and memos

English, and my work experience, I believe, make me very well-suited for
the position of Conference Manager with your hotel. I could easily arrange
to come to Mexico City for an interview in support of my application and
look forward to such an opportunity.

Sincerely yours,

Luz Lamas

Luz Lamas

PRODUCTION MANAGER

Seeking responsible person with textile engineering background for overseas position. Su-
pervise 25 people in manufacturing and dyeing
of cottons, synthetics, silks. Mfg. exp., 3–5 yrs.
supervisory exp. Degree preferred. Contact
T.M. Terry, Terry Textiles, P.O. Box 31, Jakarta, Indonesia.

Letter 2:

42 Kilauea Ave.
Honolulu, Hawaii 96816 USA
July 2, 1990

Mr. T. M. Terry
Terry Textiles
P.O. Box 31
Jakarta, Indonesia

Dear Mr. Terry:

I think I am the right person for the job because I have the right
qualifications, and they gave me a promotion because they like my
work. Also I have the right experience. The advertisement was in the
Honolulu Star Bulletin of July 1, 1990. I think you should consider my
application seriously. I have a high school diploma and I have studied
Textiles. My degree in Textiles is from Manoa Polytechnic Institute. At
school I got good grades in math, physics, and chemistry. I got my degree
in 1979. Your advertisement was for a production manager. Then I studied
other subjects related to the textile industry. I was given a promotion,
and I have been Assistant Production Manager since 1982. I like my work
very much, and I have a graduate degree in Industrial and Labor Relations
from the University of Hawaii. That was in 1984. I was born in San
Francisco, and I am bilingual in Chinese and English. I have worked for
the Topp Clothing Company since 1979. I am prepared to work hard, and I
am sure that my present employer would give me an excellent reference. I
visited relatives in Indonesia in 1979 and like Indonesia very much.

Sincerely yours,

Fred Wong

Fred Wong

6.6   *WRITING LETTERS BASED ON VISUAL INFORMATION*

A. *The shoe factory behind Lincoln Elementary School (see Figure 1) has applied for permission to expand. Read the following letter from a resident of the West End Apartments protesting the expansion and suggesting an alternative plan.*

City Planning Commission
Westfield City Council
Westfield, Michigan 48063

Dear Commissioners:

On behalf of the residents of the West End Apartments, I want to protest the proposed expansion of the Fall Shoe Factory in the area between River Road and West Street behind the Lincoln Elementary School. We oppose the expansion because:

First, the local Board of Education has filed an application to use this land as a playground for Lincoln Elementary School, which at present has no such facility. It is almost certain that the application will be granted if the money can be raised through taxes.

Second, the smoke and smells from the factory already irritate the students of the school as well as residents nearby. Enlarging the factory would only worsen this problem.

Third, there is no major highway or railroad line to the factory, and River Road is too small for the large trucks that serve the factory. Obviously, more trucks would only make traffic matters worse.

Fourth, the residents of the West End Apartments feel that a new factory building near River Road would be totally out of keeping with the architecture of the neighborhood.

We would like to suggest that the factory be allowed to expand in the direction of Main Street instead of in the direction now proposed. Main Street can handle factory traffic, and the new section of the factory would be farther away from both the school and West End Apartments.

Thank you for your attention.

Yours sincerely,

Felix Rivera
Felix Rivera

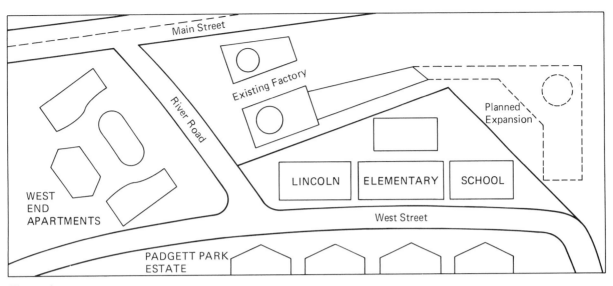

Figure 1

B. *Now, working in groups if you wish, study Figure 2. You are a resident of the townhouses and are going to write a letter to the Board of Education protesting the building of a seven-story college as proposed. Some of your objections might be:*
 — *college will block your view of the river*
 — *townhouses would have tall buildings on two sides, decreasing amount of sunlight*
 — *parking will become a problem*
 — *tennis courts and basketball courts, which are for the community, will become crowded with students*
Add additional objections if you wish, and suggest alternative solutions. Finally, write the letter.

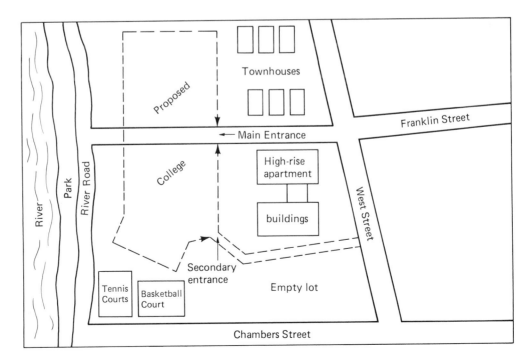

Figure 2

6.7   *PUNCTUATING: COLONS, SEMICOLONS, AND COMMAS*

A. *Notice the use of the colon in the following sentences. Discuss why it is used in each case.*

1. We need the following: three pairs of jeans, two T-shirts, and one sweatshirt.
2. The letter explained everything: She was dissatisfied with the sizing.
3. Dear Ms. Adams:

Notice the use of the semicolon in the following sentences. Discuss how each pair of sentences is related. Could the semicolon be replaced with a comma? a period?

4. At yesterday's auction the first three items went to local people; the rest went to out-of-towners.
5. Last year they were in school; this year they're in the army.
6. The equipment included a small motor, which was fitted with a transformer; two yards of wire; and a switch.

B. *Now, in groups, decide on appropriate punctuation and capitalization for the following letter:*

dear mr ahmed

    we are proud to announce the formation of a new and innovative international advertising agency business promoters international we are convinced that you will recognize our potential as an extremely effective international advertising agency we are equally convinced that you will want to choose business promoters international to plan your international advertising compaigns

    let us tell you a little about our personnel our five promoters together represent approximately 45 years of advertising experience throughout the world the far east europe the middle east latin america and the united states their language and cultural backgrounds are as varied spanish french chinese arabic and greek of course all speak and write english fluently this multilingual aspect of business promoters international is a great plus when handling the delicate matter of translating advertising slogans from one language to another to

illustrate the importance of this you need only recall the unfortunate

translation of the pepsi slogan come alive with pepsi which was trans-

lated in taiwanese as pepsi brings your ancestors back from the grave

business promoters international is committed to designing

advertising tailored to your company's marketing needs we believe in

what our name represents promoting your business throughout the world

we look forward to the opportunity of working with you

sincerely yours

brenda kostas

6.8   PRACTICING WRITING BUSINESS LETTERS AND MEMOS

Choose one of the following topics. Write:

a) A memo on the retirement (or promotion) of someone who started in a company as a clerk and gradually worked up to more and more influential positions; the person had been responsible for several creative management decisions, such as flexible working hours, child care, and an annual bonus for people who had perfect attendance at work. (Compare 6.1)

b) A reply to the memo of 6.2, accepting some suggestions and rejecting others, and making alternative suggestions.

c) Mr. Duval's reply to Mr. Dumont's letter in 6.4B, taking up each of the points and reassuring the potential client.

d) A letter of application for a specific job advertised in your local newspaper. (Compare 6.5)

e) A memo to a supervisor suggesting changes to be made in your place of work, such as rearrangement of work space, or a letter to the director of your school suggesting similar changes. You may wish to illustrate your memo or letter with a drawing. (Compare 6.6)

f) A reply to the letter in 6.7, agreeing to hire the advertising agency and describing briefly your advertising needs.

g) A memo to all the staff of a large company suggesting ways of economizing on the use of paper, electricity, water, etc.

h) A letter to a company from which you purchased merchandise explaining an error in billing or a piece of faulty or unsatisfactory merchandise.

7   Stating an opinion I

ORGANIZING IDEAS

The following sentences form an opinion essay, but they are in the wrong order. Working with a group, put them in logical order. Discuss how the underlined words and phrases help you. When you have finished, divide the sentences into paragraphs and write out the essay.

a) The elderly couple down the street from me, <u>for example</u>, spent over $20 on lottery tickets last week, and they have only their <u>meager</u> social security checks to support them.

b) I <u>only</u> wish to express my opinion, namely, that lottery games of all types should be abolished.

c) People who want to gamble would be better off in places like Las Vegas or Hong Kong where they would at least be <u>using some skill</u>.

d) I would like to express my concern at the growing number of lottery games in this country.

e) Just last month, <u>a gang of youths tried to hassle</u> people lined up to buy lottery tickets at my local newsstand, making a tremendous amount of <u>noise</u> in the attempt.

f) <u>Second</u>, while I do not object to gambling in principle, I feel that <u>this particular kind</u>, where no skill is required on the part of the player, is especially offensive and deadening to the intellect.

g) <u>In conclusion</u>, let me say that I do not wish to appear old-fashioned or anti-pleasure.

h) There are several reasons why I object to <u>this kind of gambling</u>.

i) <u>Finally</u>, the places where lottery tickets are sold often attract undesirable people to otherwise quiet neighborhoods.

j) <u>First</u>, the people who run <u>the lotteries</u> are taking substantial amounts of money away from people, many of whom are old and can least afford to lose it.

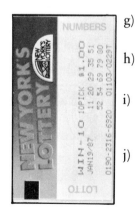

| 7.2 | **RELATING IDEAS: LINKING WORDS AND PHRASES** |

In the following essay, the linking words and phrases are left out. For numbers 1–9, choose the most appropriate words or phrases from those given below the essay. For numbers 10–16, fill in each blank with any linking word or phrase that makes sense. Look back at similar exercises in previous chapters to help you if necessary.

Living in an ethnic community is very pleasant, (1) _____ it definitely has some disadvantages. Let me explain what I mean through personal example.

(2) _____, when I came from Cuba to live in Miami, I was very happy (3) _____ all my old friends were living in the same neighborhood I was. I didn't ever feel lonely. (4) _____, if I needed help with anything, (5) _____, with the language or the subway, someone was there to help me. For me, that was very nice (6) _____ it made me feel right at home.

A year later, (7) _____, my family and I decided to move from that area in order to live near where we worked. That day I began to feel that I was living in another country, in another city, in another Miami. My first problem came (8) _____ I tried to tell the landlord of our building that our refrigerator was broken. He didn't speak Spanish, (9) _____ I didn't speak English. Little things like that made me feel unhappy and insecure, (10) _____ I did not want to go back to my own ethnic community. (11) _____ I came to realize that I was not living in my country anymore. (12) _____, I was living in a new country, (13) _____ I had to do things for myself. I had to learn a different culture, a different language, and different customs.

Living with my ethnic group was very comfortable, (14) _____, at the same time, in my opinion, it was harmful (15) _____ I didn't learn some of the essentials for survival in a foreign country, (16) _____ the language. It was an important, though painful, lesson to learn.

1. a) on the contrary   b) and   c) but   d) so
2. a) at first   b) first   c) although   d) beforehand
3. a) because of   b) besides   c) because   d) despite
4. a) however   b) besides   c) nevertheless   d) first

5. a) to begin with   b) though   c) moreover   d) for instance
6. a) even though   b) at last   c) although   d) since
7. a) however   b) but   c) although   d) for instance
8. a) as well as   b) and   c) when   d) moreover
9. a) because   b) but   c) and   d) since

| 7.3 | **SHOWING ATTITUDE** |

Two short interviews on the same topic appear below. Fill in the blanks with words from the list below that show the interviewees' attitude to what they are saying.

Should laws restrict where people can smoke?

Reply 1:

Laws (1) _____ should dictate where people can smoke.
(2) _____, I support laws that allow smoking only in one's own home or private office. For one thing, scientific research (3) _____ proves that smoking not only harms the health of smokers, it also harms the health of nonsmokers around them. Wives and children of smokers, for example, have been found to have more instances of lung cancer, ear and throat infections, and asthma than wives and children of nonsmokers. For another thing, nonsmokers must (4) _____ pay for the consequences of smoking, such as fires and increased costs of ventilation. (5) _____, we cannot depend on smokers to be considerate and respectful of the health and pocketbooks of those around them. (6) _____, for the good of all society, we need laws to tell smokers when and where to smoke.

Choices:

1. a) confidentially   b) certainly   c) perhaps   d) admittedly
2. a) in fact   b) evidently   c) presumably   d) to my surprise
3. a) eventually   b) to be honest   c) clearly   d) quite likely
4. a) in short   b) fortunately   c) unjustly   d) to tell you the truth
5. a) in theory   b) perhaps   c) unfortunately   d) unjustly
6. a) presumably   b) in my opinion   c) to my surprise   d) officially

Reply 2:

Laws should (7) _____ not restrict where people can smoke.
(8) _____, any arguments that say smoking affects the health of
nonsmokers are based on emotions, not science. (9) _____, there
is no conclusive evidence to prove that the health of wives and children of smokers is
harmed by their husbands or fathers smoking. Banning smoking in public places, like
restaurants and offices, only causes loss of income and lower productivity. It also,
(10) _____, unfairly restricts people's freedom of choice.
(11) _____, this is an issue that arouses a lot of anger on the part
of a lot of people, but, (12) _____, anger should not dictate laws.
The decision of where and when to smoke should, (13) _____, be
left to common courtesy and sense.

7. a) definitely   b) officially   c) eventually   d) in short
8. a) perhaps   b) apparently   c) as far as I'm concerned   d) literally
9. a) in theory   b) personally   c) seriously   d) as a matter of fact
10. a) I believe   b) personally   c) perhaps   d) naturally
11. a) naturally   b) by all means   c) unjustly   d) unlikely
12. a) clearly   b) presumably   c) literally   d) maybe
13. a) admittedly   b) unfortunately   c) technically   d) in my opinion

*Now write an essay giving your own opinion on this topic. You may want to use part
or all of one of the paragraphs above as an introduction. Work either individually or
in a group.*

© 1978, American Cancer Society, Inc.

7.4   COMPARING TEXTS: FIRST PARAGRAPHS

A. Below are two suggestions for the first paragraph of an essay on why it is good to live in a city. Working in groups, decide which paragraph is better organized and why. Then discuss your decision with other groups.

Choice 1:

There are various advantages to living in a large city. In the first place, there are many excellent facilities in a large city. Second, educational programs of all kinds for all ages and interests are available at all times of day and night in a city. And finally, a city offers a wide range of choices in recreation, culture, and entertainment. Moreover, there are many jobs in many fields available. These jobs pay well, offering good chances for professional advancement, and there are many interesting people to meet in a large city. Let us look at each of these points in some detail.

Choice 2:

There are various advantages to living in a large city. For one thing, there is the matter of education; there are many different kinds of excellent educational programs for all education levels and interests available at all times of night and day in a city. Then, there are cultural and recreational considerations: A city offers a wide range of choices in entertainment, recreation, and culture as well as opportunities to meet many interesting and varied people. Last but not least is the opportunity for jobs and money a city provides: Many jobs are available in a wide variety of fields, with a lot of chance for professional advancement and with higher salaries than in a small town. Let us look at each of these points in some detail.

B. *Now, working individually, write the first paragraph of an essay that holds the opposite point of view: why it is good to live in a rural area (or small town). Notice that the best paragraph in part A gives three reasons with additional details for each. Before you begin to write, you may wish to make a list of three or four reasons and then list details under each reason. This results in an outline, which may help you in organizing your first paragraph.*

Hint: If you have trouble getting ideas, here are two suggestions:
1) *Brainstorm with others in your group.*
2) *Free-write for 10 minutes to generate ideas about the topic. (Write as fast as possible. Put down whatever comes to your mind. Do not worry about being correct. This is only to get ideas.)*

C. *Optional: Either complete the essay you began in part B or complete the essay started in part A, using the paragraph you chose as the best as your first paragraph. You should discuss each reason in more detail, perhaps giving specific examples, to explain and support what you say.*

7.5   WRITING AN ESSAY BASED ON A CONVERSATION

Below is a conversation between two farmers from the United States, each with different views on farming practices. Choose one side of the argument and write an essay explaining that point of view. Before you write, organize your ideas into an outline. Your essay will appear as a guest editorial in a local newspaper.

A: Do you realize that U.S. farmers are producing 13% of the world's wheat, 25% of its corn, and 62% of the world's soybeans? Isn't that great productivity?

B: Yes, but you're not taking into account that this high productivity has its costs. We can't continue farming the way we do without damage to the topsoil, for example, or without getting deeper and deeper in debt.

A: But we're "miracle farmers." We've made farming into a big industry, and we're making money at it.

B: Yes, that's true. But I just found out that my land is losing one inch of topsoil every three years. In a few years, I'll be out of business. They tell me that planting tree belts to protect the soil from winds, and terracing* to prevent erosion, will help prevent that.   ⟫→

---

*terracing: creating level or flat pieces of ground on a hillside by raising the earth

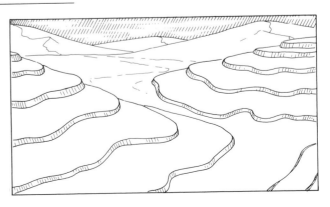

A: But trees and terracing would interfere with my big machines. I can't do that! Besides, I'm just renting my land for a few years. My biggest concern is getting the most from the land in a few years' time.

B: Another thing I learned is that by irrigating so much, the water table is being lowered. In fact, my neighbor's well just ran dry!

A: But we've *got* to irrigate to farm this dry land! If I didn't irrigate, the land would be worthless. After all, the bigger the better – the more land I farm, the more I'll produce and the more money I'll make.

B: It's been proven that bigger doesn't always mean more efficient. And you know, people used to believe this country's resources were unlimited. I think we're learning differently, now. Not only that, the fertilizers and pesticides we use are contaminating the water we drink. That could really be dangerous for health. It could cause cancer and birth defects.

A: But how can we continue to get high yields if we don't do something about insects and weeds? They'll take over our crops!

B: Well, I know someone who is pretty much taking care of weeds and insects by rotating his crops – planting a different crop each season. Of course, he has a smaller farm with smaller machinery, but, you know, he's making a profit!

A: The thing is, I don't think it's only *our* responsibility to worry about things like saving the soil and water for future generations. I think it's the government's responsibility, too, along with the agricultural experts who've been telling us to farm this way.

B: Yes, I think I agree with you about that. In the meantime, I'm going to talk to that guy who's farming less land, using less machinery and fewer chemicals, but still seeing a profit. I want to find out exactly how he does it.

7.6   WRITING AN ESSAY BASED ON VISUAL INFORMATION

Working in groups, look at the drawings below. Choose one that suggests an issue to you. Discuss the issue in the group, giving your opinions on it and reasons for those opinions. Finally, individually, write an essay in which you state your opinion and explain it.

a)

b)

c)

d)

7.7   ADDING EXAMPLES AND DETAILS

Read the short opinion essay below. Notice that it introduces a topic, states an opinion about the topic, and gives two reasons to support that opinion. However, it does not discuss the reasons in any detail.

Older people in some countries are not really appreciated by their families. Too often, their children and grandchildren do not have time to pay adequate attention to them. Many times, the older members of a family are put into a nursing home instead of being taken care of by the family. This practice of not valuing the older generation, of sometimes even ignoring them, is a disgrace. We should do everything in our power to change this phenomenon in our society, first, because ignoring the older members of our families in this way makes them feel unwanted and unloved, and second, because older people have a great deal of knowledge and experience to contribute to their families and to society.

With your group, using your own words, restate:

Writer's main point (proposition): _____

_____

Reason 1: _____

_____

Reason 2: _____

_____

Now make the essay stronger by thinking of examples and details to explain and support each of the reasons. In an outline, organize these examples and details under each reason. Then write a separate paragraph for each of the reasons. Finally, add a suitable conclusion. Your essay should have four paragraphs when you are finished.

7.8   *DEBATING ISSUES*

The following article and guest interviews appeared in the same newspaper on the same day; they all refer to the controversy about whether or not computers are good educators. After reading the interviews, write a guest editorial supporting one side of the issue. You may want to go through these steps.

Either individually or in a group:
1. *Decide your point of view about the question.*
2. *Spend 10 minutes listing ideas that support your point of view.*
3. *Choose the most important ideas.*
4. *Decide on a suitable order for the ideas.*
5. *Decide how many paragraphs your essay will have.*
6. *Write the essay using linking words and phrases where needed.*
7. *Compare your essay with those of others.*

Are computers good educators?

Computers are becoming more and more prevalent in our schools; even five-year-olds are learning how to use them. Many child development experts are worried that computers may deprive children of their childhood by pushing them into formal education too early in life. Others feel that computers do not replace child play; they simply enhance it by freeing the imagination, for example in allowing children to write stories on the computer. Most people would probably agree, however, that it is too soon to know how computers will affect the education of children.

Interviews: Should computers be encouraged in schools?

Reply 1: We've had many other fads in education, like tape recorders and television, and these things were not the salvation of our schools. The computer is just another fad. It'll die out in a few years, you'll see.

Reply 2: Educators are too conservative to use computers wisely in the schools. So far, computers have been used mostly for drill work, and doing drills is not the best way to learn. I'm against using computers in schools unless some more imaginative uses are found for them.

Reply 3: Using the computer to write can be very freeing for children. Because they do not have to worry about holding a pencil and shaping letters, they can concentrate on what they are writing, and their stories can become very imaginative. I think using computers for writing is very worthwhile. Let's keep them.

Reply 4: Children should learn the basics of computers simply because computers are affecting our everyday world in so many ways. We don't want to raise computer illiterates. We'd better let children become acquainted with them in school.

Reply 5: If you start children with computers too early in life, the computers will control the children. Children need to be active, to be outdoors; they don't need to be silently hooked to a computer.

Reply 6: As long as children get a balanced education, I see nothing wrong with encouraging children to learn to use computers in school. Working with a computer can help you to learn math and accounting. And if writing on the computer helps you become a better reader, what's wrong with that?

7.9   *PUNCTUATING: WHEN AND WHEN NOT TO*

A. *In groups, discuss the use of punctuation or the lack of punctuation in the following sentences.*

1a. Health experts say to eat a balanced diet.
 b. Health experts say, "Eat a balanced diet."

2a. They ask you if you know about nutrition.
 b. They ask, "Do you know about nutrition?"

3a. They give you plenty of information on nutrition if you are ignorant about it.
 b. If you are ignorant about nutrition, they give you plenty of information on it.

4.   It is obvious that they want you to follow their advice.

5a. Most people, therefore, try to do so if they can.
 b. Therefore, most people try to do so if they can.
 c. Therefore, if they can, most people try to do so.

B. *There are some mistakes in the use of punctuation and capital letters in the following essay. Edit the essay by correcting the mistakes.*

Poor people and Nutrition

Nutrition is for people who have the power to buy any kind of food they want, food is at their doorstep and if they do not have the money the government protects and feeds them. These people can afford to take care of their bodies, and their appearance through good nutrition

However in my Country Diet and Nutrition are not popular subjects, you cannot talk about proper diet and nutrition to most people here, because the words have no meaning for the masses. Only a tiny group of Privileged People can afford to understand these words,

People live from day to day, they eat whatever they can get in any day. Sometimes they have one meal a day and they wake up the next day with nothing to eat. There is a lack of everything and there is no money to buy anything

We are not protected by the Government, we eat only what we can provide for ourselves and most of us have no money. Therefore when a Doctor says "watch your diet and think about nutrition the words are empty. They have no meaning. we eat what we have for each day, we cannot afford Nutrition.

| 7.10 | **PRACTICING WRITING OPINION ESSAYS** |

Choose one of the following topics. Write:

a) An essay objecting to some form of recreation, such as gambling or card playing or a particular sport, or to a particular recreation area in your neighborhood, such as an amusement park. (Compare 7.1 and 7.3)

b) An essay discussing the advantages and disadvantages of two different places you have lived (compare 7.2 and 7.4) or two different life-styles.

c) An essay that explains another person's opinion about an issue that is important to you; interview the person first. (Compare 7.5)

d) An essay giving your opinion on how old people are treated in your society. (Compare 7.7)

e) An essay on a particular educational practice, such as the value of practical training in a college career program, or the value of on-the-job training courses for improving particular job skills. (Compare 7.8)

f) An essay that gives your opinion about a major difference you notice between your culture and another culture. (Compare 7.9)

g) An essay that describes an important lesson you learned or a change you made in your life, giving your opinion about that experience.

8 Stating an opinion II

ORGANIZING IDEAS

The following sentences form an opinion essay, but they are in the wrong order. Working with a group, put them in logical order. Discuss how the underlined words help you. When you have finished, divide the sentences into paragraphs and write out the essay.

a) For another thing, children whose mothers work are enriched by their mother's experience and knowledge of the work world; these children get more than just their father's view of the world.

b) In fact, I believe that children benefit when their mothers work.

c) You often hear people say, "A woman's place is in the home."

d) My brother's children, for example, were in daycare centers from infancy to kindergarten, and they became very mature at a young age.

e) I am one of those who believe that mothers are not neglecting their responsibilities by working outside the home.

f) Finally, and quite obviously, the children of working mothers have the economic advantages gained from their mother's income.

g) Others, however, find this notion old-fashioned in today's world of tight budgets and good child-care facilities.

h) Their daycare experience was a definite plus for them.

i) For one thing, children who are cared for by babysitters or in daycare centers gain independence, maturity, and social skills more quickly than those cared for by their mother.

j) In short, as long as children are well cared for, I'm for mothers who work.

k) Many traditionalists support this statement, saying that a woman's first responsibility is to her husband and children.

8.2   RELATING IDEAS: LINKING WORDS AND PHRASES

In the following essay, the linking words and phrases are left out. For numbers 1–12, choose the most appropriate words or phrases from those given below. For numbers 13–18, fill in each blank with any word or phrase that makes sense. Look back at similar exercises in previous chapters to help you if necessary.

Every day we hear about the problem of hunger in Africa. Many authorities state causes, (1) _____ drought and overpopulation. They (2) _____ suggest solutions, (3) _____ food aid and population control.

It is true that such realities as drought and overpopulation worsen the problem of hunger in Africa. (4) _____, these realities are not the real cause of Africa's famine. The real culprit is poverty, (5) _____ only by doing something about poverty itself can we solve the hunger problem in Africa.

I am not suggesting that we ignore the problems of drought and overpopulation.

>>>→

(6) _____, I believe we should study them carefully in order to learn what lies behind them. Let us look, (7) _____, at drought.

Insufficient rainfall is a problem for farmers all over the world,

(8) _____ it is only the truly poor who die from it. How,

(9) _____, did Africans become so poor? In the past several hundred years, with the help of European colonizers, the best farm lands were taken and planted in cash crops for export, with profits going to a few of the wealthy.

(10) _____ , there has not been enough food produced for the poor majority, (11) _____ it is these already hungry people who are so affected by drought. Since food aid treats symptoms, not causes, I suggest that the only long-lasting solution to this problem lies, not in food aid,

(12) _____ in revising Africa's farming practices.

(13) _____, let's look at the second problem authorities mention, (14) _____, overpopulation. It is true that Africa's population growth rate is higher than that of any other continent.

(15) _____, having many children is logical for African farmers, who need a lot of workers for the family farm and who know that one out of three of these children will die before adulthood. Studies from all over the world show that the best way to raise living standards is to lower birth rates.

(16) _____ , when African parents can be sure their children will survive and that they can earn a decent living, they will not need to have so many of them.

(17) _____, I suggest that when we hear the words *drought* and *overpopulation* in connection with famine in Africa, let's keep in mind the real enemy, (18) _____, poverty.

1. a) either   b) consequently   c) likewise   d) such as
2. a) also   b) but   c) for example   d) nevertheless
3. a) and   b) such as   c) besides   d) on the other hand
4. a) and   b) finally   c) because   d) however
5. a) or   b) when   c) and   d) anyway
6. a) on the contrary   b) at least   c) moreover   d) then
7. a) such as   b) first   c) however   d) though
8. a) even though   b) by the way   c) but   d) then
9. a) then   b) however   c) for instance   d) well
10. a) on the contrary   b) consequently   c) second   d) at last
11. a) when   b) and   c) because   d) or
12. a) but   b) and   c) by the way   d) though

| **8.3** | **SHOWING ATTITUDE** |

Two short interviews appear below. They both answer the question, "Does watching violence on TV affect society?" Fill in the blanks with words and phrases that show the two writers' attitudes to what they are saying. Choose the best expression from those given below.

Reply 1:

(1) _____, what one sees on TV affects how one acts, both positively and negatively. For example, thousands of children got library cards a few years ago after seeing the character Fonzie get a library card on the TV show *Happy Days*. This is (2) _____ evidence of a positive effect of TV on viewers. At the same time, (3) _____, we also see proof of TV's negative influence on viewers. One such example was the boy who jumped out a window, trying to fly, after seeing *Superman* on TV. (4) _____, psychologists have issued a resolution on the issue, saying, "Viewing television violence may lead to increases in aggressive attitudes, values, and behavior, particularly in children." (5) _____, that's proof enough for me. (6) _____, TV violence (7) _____ affects society.

1. a) technically   b) undoubtedly   c) apparently   d) officially
2. a) certainly   b) frankly   c) ideally   d) honestly
3. a) in theory   b) confidentially   c) even worse   d) of course
4. a) generally speaking   b) naturally   c) in fact   d) in short
5. a) literally   b) frankly   c) to my surprise   d) unfortunately
6. a) in my opinion   b) presumably   c) admittedly   d) perhaps
7. a) naturally   b) frankly   c) maybe   d) definitely

Reply 2:

(8) _____, this case of TV violence affecting viewers has not been sufficiently proven, and there are (9) _____ experts who would agree with me. (10) _____, an article in the *Psychological Bulletin* in September of 1984 stated a similar opinion, saying, "There is little convincing evidence that in natural settings viewing television violence causes people to be more aggressive." (11) _____, I watch a lot of television,

⫸→

including shows with violence, and I have never found myself showing aggressive behavior as a result. (12) _____, these accusations against TV are simply distracting us from getting at the real causes of violence, those related to economic, political, and social problems. (13) _____, let's quit condemning TV.

8. a) literally   b) as far as I'm concerned   c) naturally   d) fortunately
9. a) certainly   b) frankly   c) personally   d) officially
10. a) roughly speaking   b) literally   c) as a matter of fact
      d) generally speaking
11. a) personally   b) in theory   c) to my surprise   d) unfortunately
12. a) obviously   b) fortunately   c) in my opinion   d) confidentially
13. a) generally speaking   b) in short   c) unlikely   d) presumably

Now write an essay giving your own opinion on this topic. You may want to use part or all of one of the above paragraphs as a beginning. Work either individually or in a group.

8.4   WRITING FIRST AND LAST PARAGRAPHS

A. *Look at the last paragraphs of the essays shown in 7.1, 7.2, 8.1, and 8.2. Notice different ways to conclude argumentative or opinion essays. Then write a concluding paragraph for the following essay.*

Large cities like New York City, Mexico City, and Tokyo have enormous problems with crowded streets, congested traffic, and noise and air pollution. These problems could be at least partially alleviated if private cars were not allowed in the centers of these cities on weekdays.

Every day thousands of vehicles fill the streets of large cities, especially during rush hours. Very often, the large numbers of cars, buses, and trucks cause so much congestion that traffic stops. No vehicle can move in any direction, and no one can get anywhere. These problems could be eased if autos were not allowed on the streets of cities with such problems. Instead, people could use public transportation or, if necessary, taxis. Traffic would flow much more freely that way, and people could get to their destinations in a reasonable length of time. The streets of some large cities are not capable of accommodating the number of vehicles that now try to use them.

Parking is another problem. There are not enough parking facilities in many cities, and when cars try to park on the streets, there is not enough room for traffic. Banning private cars from these cities, at least during the work week, would take care of the terrible parking situations that exist now.

Finally, the traffic in large cities adds to problems of air and noise pollution. If cars were banned, there would be fewer vehicles dirtying the air and disturbing the peace.

(LAST PARAGRAPH MISSING)

B. Look at the first paragraph of the essays in 7.1, 7.2, 8.1, 8.4A, and the first two paragraphs of 8.2. Notice some different ways to begin argumentative essays. Then write an introductory paragraph for the following essay.

(FIRST PARAGRAPH MISSING)

There are millions of people today who are able and eager to work but are unemployed. In this time of high unemployment, putting job satisfaction before job security is a luxury most people can't afford. For example, a friend of mine gave up a secure secretarial job to find work that was more rewarding and exciting. That was five years ago. She is still not employed full-time. If she wanted to return to her old job, she would no longer be qualified, since the company now requires computer skills. She risked job security to look for more interesting work, and she lost. She's not only having a hard time making ends meet, but she also has none of the ordinary job benefits, such as medical insurance or a pension plan.

I know someone else who is working for a small company doing administrative work. A few years ago she was very tempted to change careers and look for a different job. However, she decided instead to look for ways to change her job. She asked her supervisor for more responsibilities in areas that interested her. Her supervisor agreed, and today my friend is very happy in her work. She chose to try to alter her job so that it became more challenging to her instead of looking for other work.

I believe that it's wiser these days for people to look for challenges and changes within their present jobs rather than trying to find different work and risk not having a job at all. There is a need in all of us to feel and be secure, and having and keeping a job is one very important aspect of personal security.

People lined up in an unemployment compensation office

8.5   SELECTING AND ORDERING INFORMATION

The beginning of an opinion essay appears below. Following it is a list of points that could be included in the rest of the essay. Working in groups, decide which points to include and why others should be left out. Then group the points into paragraphs and write each paragraph, adding linking words and/or sentences where necessary. Finally, add a conclusion if needed.

Many psychologists say that aggressive competitive sports are a way for both players and viewers to let off steam, to relieve frustration, and thus to lessen aggressiveness. In fact, many people see international games, if not as a substitute for warfare, at least as a way to build good will and understanding among nations. However, there are other psychologists who argue that participation in aggressive sports does not lessen feelings of aggression; on the contrary, it builds them up. They say further that the acts of aggression and violence that often occur on the playing field affect the fans as well. In other words, violence in sports can cause violence in people watching those sports. From what I have seen and read, I agree that brutality in sports can increase chances for brutality among fans.

Choose from these points:

A person in a large crowd watching a sporting event feels anonymous in that crowd and therefore feels less inhibited about showing aggressive behavior when excited about something that happens on the playing field.

Sigmund Freud believed that sports that have a lot of physical contact help both players and spectators to get rid of feelings of aggression.

Most sports contests are peaceful affairs for most people.

Fans get more excited when watching rough sports like soccer, hockey, or boxing than they do when watching sports like golf, gymnastics, or swimming.

Research with high school and college athletes finds that students who participate in more aggressive sports like hockey or soccer show anger more quickly than those who participate in sports like swimminng, where competitors do not come near each other.

Young people especially tend to imitate sports heroes, and if they see those heroes punching one another in a boxing match, they may try to do the same.

I have often seen shouting matches and even fights among spectators at college soccer games.

Sometimes sports fans drink, and this can contribute to violence and rowdiness.

Violence among sports fans is only an indication of increasing violence in society.

In Ancient Rome, spectators supported one of two teams of charioteers, and these two groups of fans often had fights.

Social problems like unemployment and extreme nationalism may be major reasons for violence among sports fans.

8.6   COMPARING TEXTS

Below are two essays. Compare them and decide which is better written. Consider these aspects of good style and organization: relevance of ideas, connected sentences, logical grouping of ideas, and good paragraphing. Then rewrite the poorly written essay.

Essay 1:

```
            Down With Beauty Contests

     Young women who participate in beauty contests are
helping to keep alive an outdated view of women: that
a woman's most important asset is how she looks. I'm
against beauty contests for this reason.
     Women have been working very hard through the years
to change their image. They have been trying to prove
that the value of a woman does not lie solely in her
beauty. The world is just beginning to recognize that
women are as intelligent, capable, wise, and strong in
character as men are, and that there are virtues more
important than looks when judging people. When women
focus attention on their bodies by competing for top
prizes in beauty contests, they encourage people to
value them for their beauty alone. It is demeaning to
say that beauty alone determines one's worth.
     Beauty contests not only encourage spectators to
judge women by their appearance, but they encourage
this attitude in the contestants as well. These young
```

>>>→

women spend months dieting to become the "right" size and learning how to dress, wear makeup, and walk just right so that some judges will call them beautiful. I think it's great for a woman to feel good about her appearance, but looks shouldn't become an obsession. There are too many other, more important, concerns in a young woman's life: learning, developing friendships, and preparing for a career and perhaps a family.

As long as there are beauty contests, women won't be fully appreciated as well-rounded, complex human beings. Let's abolish beauty contests now!

Essay 2:

No More Video Games

One of the most popular video games is something called Pac-Man. They are nothing but a waste of time. Teenagers are spending far too much time and money in video arcades these days. They are a waste of money. Teenagers could be doing more valuable things than playing video games. Video games should be done away with. They are a waste of energy. Teenagers should be doing valuable things like reading, studying, and going to concerts and museums.

These places are filled with smoke and foul air. Doing physical activities in the open air would be much healthier for teenagers. I am sure they would enjoy it more, too.

Young people could spend their time in far healthier places than inside video arcades. A lot of money is spent by teenagers on these games. The lights are often dim and the games are noisy, which damages people's eyes and ears. They think nothing of spending ten or twenty dollars in an afternoon or evening just to have the satisfaction of sometimes beating an electronic machine. I don't enjoy playing these games at all.

Teenagers would be much better off without the temptation these places provide. Playing video games does not allow people to use any of their natural creativity. There is also no opportunity for physical exercise, something young people are sadly lacking these days. Why, most teenagers can't even run a mile, and adults are in even worse shape.

Video arcades should be banned from our cities and towns.

8.7	***ADDING EXAMPLES AND DETAILS***

Read the short opinion essay below. Notice that it introduces a topic, states an opinion about the topic, and gives three reasons to support that opinion. However, it does not discuss the reasons in any detail.

In the days of the early settlement of places like North America and Australia, it was necessary for settlers to share resources. One family could not afford to own an expensive plow or buttermaker on their own. Instead, expensive equipment was bought cooperatively, each family paying part of the cost and sharing in its use.

There are many families all over the world today that are in the same situation. They can't afford costly items such as a car or a computer, or even a stepladder or a radio. These families should consider cooperative buying. Almost anything one might want to buy can be jointly owned. There are several advantages to this: It will cost less than buying on your own, and there will be fewer worries about upkeep. Also, if people are careful about their co-op partners, they will develop some good friendships as a result.

With your group, using your own words, restate:

WRITER'S MAIN POINT (PROPOSITION): _____

_____

REASON 1: _____

_____

REASON 2: _____

_____

REASON 3: _____

_____

Now make the essay stronger by thinking of examples and details to explain and support each of the reasons. Then write a separate paragraph for each of the reasons, including your examples and details in each paragraph. Finally, add a suitable conclusion. Your essay should have five paragraphs when you are finished.

8.8   *DEBATING ISSUES*

The following article and guest interviews appeared in the same newspaper on the same day; they all refer to the controversy about whether or not people over the age of 70 should be forced to retire. After reading the material below, write a guest editorial supporting one side of the issue. You may want to go through these steps.

Either individually or in a group:
1. *Decide your point of view about the question.*
2. *Spend 10 minutes listing ideas that support your point of view.*
3. *Choose the most important ideas.*
4. *Decide on a suitable order for the ideas.*
5. *Decide how many paragraphs your essay will have.*
6. *Write the essay using linking words and phrases where needed.*
7. *Compare your essay with those of others.*

Should those over 70 be forced to retire?

In some countries laws now protect people between the ages of 40 and 70 from age discrimination. But once people reach 71, their employers can ask them to retire. Should these older people be allowed to keep working if they can do the job? Many people think so. Others disagree.

Interviews: Should there be a mandatory retirement age?

Reply 1: If there is no mandatory retirement, it will be hard for employers to plan ahead, since they will not be certain how long their older employees will continue to work.

Reply 2: Older people should have the right to choose when they want to retire. They should not be victims of age discrimination.

Reply 3: If people are not forced to retire at a certain age, productivity will be lowered simply because so many of the nation's workers will be old. Older people are less productive than younger workers.

Reply 4: Some people say that if older workers continue to work, they delay younger workers from being promoted. I disagree. There is a report that says that raising the retirement age would only delay promotions by, at the most, six months. Six months is not a serious delay of promotion.

Reply 5: By continuing to work if they wish, older people will contribute a considerable amount of money to Social Security, which will be of great help to the economy. Retirement costs us a lot of money, and letting people work longer would lessen those costs.

Reply 6: Without forced retirement, older people will hang on to their positions and prevent younger workers from moving up the work ladder.   »»→

Younger workers should be given the opportunity to advance in their fields and not be stopped by older workers.

Reply 7: Older people are dependable and experienced as workers and can offer a lot to their employers.

8.9   *PUNCTUATING: WHEN AND WHEN NOT TO*

The letter below appeared in a Letters to the Editor column of a small-town newspaper. It needs proper punctuation, capitalization, and paragraphing. Work in groups to do this.

Dear editor

I am writing this letter to complain about the morrison county highway department neglecting to repair county route 10 between the towns of wadena and st. cloud many cars have been seriously damaged by bumps in the road in fact people are even afraid to take route 10 to st cloud for shopping because they fear for the welfare of their cars unfortunately there are more serious problems than cars people's health has also been in danger there have been several seriously ill patients for example who had to be moved from riverview hospital in wadena to franklin memorial hospital in st cloud the condition of the wadena–st cloud road has forced ambulances to take a longer route through the town of brainerd this has been an inconvenience an added expense and at times even a danger for these patients they ask such questions as these cant we do something about repairing route 10 soon so we can return to our homes in the most direct and comfortable way do we have to wait for a serious accident before getting route 10 repaired we *all* need this road repaired can't the highway department do it soon

a concerned citizen of wadena

Optional: Discuss these questions:

What is the opinion of the letter writer?
Would a letter like this be appropriate for your town or city newspaper? Why or why not?
Would *any* letter complaining about something be appropriate to send to your local newspaper? Why or why not?
What would be some appropriate topics to write to your local newspaper about?

8.10   *PRACTICING WRITING OPINION ESSAYS*

Choose one of the topics below. Write:

a) An essay on the advantages or disadvantages of being the oldest child in a family, or the advantages or disadvantages of being single (or married). (Compare 8.1)

b) An essay that gives a different viewpoint than the one expressed in 8.2 about the problem of hunger in Africa, or an essay on a similar serious problem in your country, or on an issue that is in the news. (Compare 8.2)

c) An essay that explains another person's point of view about an issue related to a type of recreation or education; interview the person first. (Compare 8.3)

d) An essay giving your opinion about one solution to a problem in your city or neighborhood. (Compare 8.4A)

e) An essay giving your opinion about job security or another job-related issue, such as health benefits or retirement plans. (Compare 8.4B)

f) An essay giving your opinion on young people and beauty contests, video games, rock music, or other such issues. (Compare 8.6)

g) An essay making a suggestion, such as a way to save money or a way to overcome shyness. (Compare 8.7)

h) An essay giving your opinion about this statement: Anyone who is guilty of murdering another person should die for that act. Capital punishment is the only way to convince would-be murderers not to commit such a crime.

i) An essay giving your opinion on fathers caring for children, or on divorced fathers having custody of their children.

j) An essay giving your opinion about an environmental issue.